THE MASSACHUSETTS BAY COMPANY
AND ITS PREDECESSORS

THE MASSACHUSETTS BAY COMPANY AND ITS PREDECESSORS

BY

FRANCES ROSE-TROUP, F. R. Hist. Soc.

Author of "THE WESTERN REBELLION OF 1549," "LOST CHAPELS
OF EXETER," "THE LADY OF THE ISLES," ETC.

CLEARFIELD

Originally published
New York, 1930

Reprinted for
Clearfield Company, Inc. by
Genealogical Publishing Co., Inc.
Baltimore, Maryland
2002

International Standard Book Number: 0-8063-5136-5

Made in the United States of America

FOREWORD

THIS account of the three interrelated companies was the outcome of other work—it was necessary to understand their formation and history in order to make clear a certain point. No history of the Massachusetts Bay Company could be found and the original documents not being accessible to me, I was obliged to depend upon printed sources. What had been written about the companies was, in view of more recent discoveries, obsolete and not wholly reliable. S. F. Haven in 1850 published in the *American Antiquarian Society Transactions* the records of the Company up to 1630. N. B. Shurtleff also printed these in the *Massachusetts Records* in 1853, and some missing leaves were found and transcribed by Haven, and printed in the same *Transactions*. It is time that some competent student edited these early records of the Massachusetts Bay Company, using the manuscript material in the State Archives, giving particulars of the inserted passages, usually in different hands, and adding explanatory notes from other sources. Such an edition would doubtless solve certain puzzling entries, and certainly would make more easy the work of others who, like myself, seek to elucidate the early history of Massachusetts, which has not heretofore received due attention.

I am deeply indebted to Dr. Charles E. Banks for

valuable information given me and for the great assistance rendered in seeing this book through the press, a matter I could not attend to personally because of my residence in England.

F. R.-T.

Ottery St. Mary,
Devon, England.

CONTENTS

ix

THE MASSACHUSETTS BAY COMPANY AND ITS PREDECESSORS

I

THE THREE COMPANIES

THE early history of the Massachusetts Bay Company has never been fully elucidated; the few records remaining have frequently been misinterpreted, causing confusion so that the course of events is not clearly understood. It may lead to a better conception of the state of affairs and how they developed if the facts revealed by recent research are set out, the available material coordinated, and an opinion expressed upon the result. To understand the situation it will be necessary to deal with three companies: The Dorchester Company, The New England Company, and The Massachusetts Bay Company, all of which had their share in the establishment of the colony of Massachusetts Bay. The inception of the Dorchester Company was in a great measure the result of events upon the Plymouth Plantation, so these require consideration.

The Order in Council granting a patent of incorporation to the "Adventurers of the Northern Colony of Vir-

1

ginia," afterwards known as "The Council for New England," dated 23 July, 1620, assigned to this company the territory lying between latitudes 40° and 48°, formerly under the control of the Virginia Company; the Great Patent was issued on 3 November following, a date of importance in connection with the Pilgrim Fathers. These exiles at Leyden had applied in 1617 to the Virginia Company for permission to settle within its territory, but had failed to satisfy the Council as to their religious tenets; further efforts made later resulted in the departure of the *Mayflower* on 6 September, 1620.

The Virginia Company Records inform us that two grants were issued, one on 19 June, 1619, to John Wyncob, "commended to the Company by the Earle of Lincolne;"[1] the other seven months later, 2 February, 1619/20, to John Peirce.[2] Bradford states that in accordance with the advice of their friends, "a patent was not taken in the name of any of their owne but in the name of Mr. John Wyncob."[3] They were well aware that, after their previous failure, it would be difficult, if not impossible, for one of the exiles to obtain it, so they adopted what a carping critic might call a subterfuge. As Wyncob did not carry out his intention of emigrating, his patent, which "cost them such labour and charges," was never used.

They tried again, using John Peirce as their instrument: "this was he in whose name their '*firste patente*' was taken by reason of acquaintance and some alliance that

[1] *Records*, I, p. 221.
[2] *Ibid.*, p. 223.
[3] Bradford, *History*, ed. Ford, I, p. 94.

some of their friends had with him." [4] Apparently Bradford had forgotten the Wyncob episode when he described this as their "firste patente." Their third patent was obtained in 1629/30.

It was under Peirce's patent that they sailed, but by the time they landed on the coast of Massachusetts the division of jurisdiction had taken place and this was considered to have invalidated their patent. Mr. Worthington C. Ford writes in a note to Bradford's *History*, "The complication was explained to [Thomas] Weston by letters sent in the *Mayflower*, which returned to England in May [1621]. He [Peirce] then applied to the newly recognized Council for New England. Emboldened by his [Gorges's] success in overcoming the opposition to his company [the Council for New England] Gorges and his associates issued their first patent on June 1st, 1621, to Peirce and his associates." [5]

This patent, in the form of an indenture, allowed the establishment of a settlement, under certain conditions, within the territory under the jurisdiction of the Council for New England, and incidentally provided that if the undertakers and planters had the land they selected surveyed at their own costs within seven years, [6] they might exchange this indenture for a real patent covering the specified territory. The bearing of this proviso on this and on another occasion is important but has not been fully recognized. Emphasis must be laid on the fact that

---

[4] *Ibid.*, p. 306.
[5] *Ibid.*, p. 234, note. I have placed names in brackets to make the matter clear.
[6] H. L. Osgood, *American Colonies in the 17th Century*, I, p. 116, says that "if *after* seven years the request was presented, the grantees should be incorporated."

this and other indentures were issued to a person named
and his associates unnamed, and that when the requirements of the indenture had been fulfilled, in order to obtain a patent it was necessary to take out "letters of
association," naming all those associated with the appli-
cant for the patent. Such letters were in due course taken
out by Peirce on 20 April, 1623, by which he made the
Plymouth Adventurers jointly interested with himself [7] in
the lands taken over under the indenture of 1 June, 1621.
He then, as had been agreed, surrendered his indented
half of the document to the Council. Bradford accuses
Peirce of acting against the interests of the Plymouth
men and to his own advantage, by obtaining in his own
name a "deed pole" to himself, his heirs, associates and
assigns relating to the same land, to which the planters
said they were not privy.[8] But attention should be called
to the inclusion of his associates in this deed.

This led to a heated dispute, Peirce repudiating the
claim that he was under any such obligation to the Adventurers, while they had Peirce arrested under unusual
circumstances. In the end the Council for New England
acted as arbitrators, giving the Pilgrims the land they
occupied and leaving the remainder of the territory to
Peirce to deal with as he pleased.[9] The latter's terrible
misfortunes were attributed by the Plymouth Governor
to the hand of God as a punishment for his underhand

---

[7] In a letter, assigned by Ford to February—April, 1623, John
Peirce wrote to those at Plymouth: "And for the leters of association, by the next ship we send, I hope you shall receive satisfaction;
in the meantime whom you admite I will approve." Bradford,
History, ed. Ford, I, p. 271.

[8] *Records of the Council for New England* (Deane), p. 43.

[9] *Ibid.,* p. 45.

dealings, forgetful that Peirce's name had been used as a cover for their own purposes. This quarrel had a considerable influence upon the establishment of another colony in Massachusetts.[10]

A similar indenture to that obtained by Peirce is found in the Sheffield Patent, with like conditions, and this may be inferred also in other cases, such as the Robert Gorges grant, the Bushrod licence, and quite possibly in the "Rosewell grant" of 19 March, 1627/8.

Another and more important matter, leading to the formation of a settlement on the North Shore, was the dangerous religious opinions which certain Plymouth Adventurers believed were held by those in charge of their colony, and of which they disapproved. Bradford frequently refers to the falling away of Adventurers and

[10] The reader will be able to form his own judgment on reading the details of the lawsuits given in a note by Mr. Ford. W. R. Scott, *Joint Stock Companies*, II, p. 309, thinks Peirce has been subject to somewhat severe comment, "but as far as can be judged, without good reason. From all that is known of the methods of the Council, no patent was obtainable from it without a consideration being paid, and since the Plymouth Adventurers, even at this time, were in want of funds, it is by no means improbable that Peirce safeguarded himself by refusing to give a complete title until he had been reimbursed. The adventurers accordingly agreed to pay him £500 for his interest, whereupon application was made to the Council which recognized the Plymouth colony as entitled to the greater part of the patent granted to Peirce." There appears to be no evidence that 500li was ever paid for Peirce's patent; true, Sherley says he valued it at that sum and Ford, in the Table of Contents of Bradford's *History*, says it was purchased, but Peirce declared that he never received any payment. Sherley only says they got the patent from him with great trouble. Goodwin, *Pilgrim Republic*, p. 238, says it was not paid and adds: "Dr. Prince unfortunately stated that the bargain *was* made, and historians generally repeat the error;" in part payment of the Plymouth claim Peirce "surrendered his stock as an adventurer and assigned his patent to the Company." The rest of the debt was never received, nor does it appear that the patent had any definite value assigned to it in the transfer.

Sherley's letters show that considerable opposition was evinced by certain of them to the migration of Robinson and the other exiles at Leyden. Merchants holding Puritan opinions which differed from those of the colonists, might well recoil from an enterprise now becoming obnoxious to the ecclesiastical authorities, and likely to lead to their appearance in the spiritual courts. Before long defections occurred and a concerted movement developed, ending in a proposal to break off the existing agreement. Certain emigrants sent out to the plantation "on their particular" were not satisfied with affairs at Plymouth. Bradford says they expected too much and were not weaned from home comforts; he was glad when a number of them returned to England,[11] but he apparently did not anticipate that they would complain to the Adventurers and thus strengthen the growing faction. Their complaints were embodied in a letter sent to Plymouth which Bradford summarizes, adding his answers. Many reasons given were frivolous, such as the presence of foxes, wolves, mosquitoes, &c., but the first four complaints, placed at the head of the list as most important, related to religious matters. These with their answers may be briefly stated thus:

1. Diversity about religion. Bradford denies the existence of any such diversity.
2. Neglect of family duties on the Sabbath. That is not allowed, "we wish themselves had given better example."[12]

[11] Bradford, *Letter* of September, 1623.

[12] Mr. Ford suggests that this was connected with the act for the "better observance of the Sabbath," which King James held prevented poor labourers from taking their ease on Sunday. This hardly seems to apply.

8. Want of both sacraments.   This was admitted but was due
   to the lack of a pastor, which grieved the planters.
4. Children not catechized or taught to read.   Planters instruct their own children but they hope to have a school-
   master.   [This complaint probably referred to the Church
   catechism which was not taught.] [13]

In the ship bringing these complaints came Lyford,
a minister, sent apparently by the dissatisfied Adventurers
to report on the state of religious affairs; Bradford considered him a spy.   Among the charges subsequently
brought against him was the administration of the sacraments according to the ritual of the Book of Common
Prayer,[14] and in one of his letters to the Adventurers he
commiserates the poor souls in Plymouth who could not
have the sacraments administered to them because they
had "no ministry here since they came but such as may
be performed by any of you," a statement which shows
that the Rev. John White could not have been one of the
Adventurers addressed.[15]

It can only be inferred that the "rigid separation" of
the Plymouth Planters was not acceptable to the dissatisfied Adventurers, and from subsequent events it will become
evident that the question of religion had a very great influence upon their decision to "break away" from their
agreement.   Yet some of those who signed the deed of
sale do not appear to have been wholly in sympathy with
the Puritan element in the colony on the other side of the
Bay, but, as will be seen, when the East Anglian element

[13] Bradford, *History*, ed. Ford, I, p. 362.
[14] *Ibid.*, I, p. 395.
[15] *Ibid.*, p. 362.   Those who signed the deed of sale to the Planters
were, as far as is known, mostly merchants, but the John White
there occurring was probably "the Counsellor," afterwards a member of the Dorchester Company.

became paramount some of these joined the Massachusetts Bay Company, e.g. Thomas Goffe, appointed
Deputy Governor by the charter of 1628/9, John Revel,
mentioned in the Records on July, 1629, appointed an
"Undertaker" 1 December following, Samuel Sharpe, employed earlier in a subordinate capacity by Cradock and
by the Company, elected an Assistant 25 October, 1629.

Another Plymouth Adventurer, Richard Andrewes, was
closely associated with the Bay Company. Winthrop, 25
July, 1630, refers to some thirty pounds which he
promised to lend "to us" at Hampton, and Humfry
brought over, in 1634, his gift of sixteen heifers to the
ministers and the poor, while three-quarters of the sum
due to him from the Plymouth Planters was to be given
to the poor of the Bay, though the Plymouth men did not
pay this until 1643.[16]

Robert Keaynes, another Plymouth Adventurer, was
one of the English Adventurers of the Bay Company to
whom a letter was addressed; he emigrated to Boston in
1635, where his name was prominent in the well-known
"sow" case.

[16] See Winthrop, *History of New England,* I, pp. 374 and 136;
Bradford, *History,* ed. Ford, II, pp. 289 and 338. Although
Andrewes sold out his interest in the Plymouth adventure in 1621,
he, with Sherley, Beauchamp, and Hatherly, acted as agents for
the Plantation; after certain shady transactions, for which Sherley
was chiefly responsible, and the defection of Beauchamp and of
Hatherly, Andrewes claimed a large sum from the Planters, which
they declared had already been paid to the partners. In this dispute Andrewes accused the Planters of conduct "unbecoming fair-
dealing men, who make not so much profession to walk according
to the rule of the gospel as they" and claimed that he had been
kept out of his money for fourteen years. Mr. Ford's complete ex-
oneration of the Pilgrim Fathers can hardly be accepted as it is
based on the statements given by Bradford in his own defence, and
the evidence of his opponents is not set forth.

The transfer of their interest in colonizing schemes by these six Plymouth Adventurers to the new enterprise in Massachusetts Bay at a time when the Puritan element had been to a large extent eliminated, suggests that they themselves were merely "tending towards Separation" and that when a movement in that direction was made by the introduction of the East Anglian party they found themselves sufficiently in sympathy to join the scheme under its new leaders.

II

THE DORCHESTER COMPANY

WITH only the information we possess it is impossible to state definitely which John White heads the list of Plymouth Adventurers in 1629. It has been pointed out that the well-known rector of Dorchester could not have been among those addressed by Lyford, and it will be noticed that no one known to have been a clergyman occurs in the list, nor would one, in those dangerous days, have sought prominence by heading it. Apart from these negative reasons subsequent events show that he was so far opposed to the Plymouth opinions, of which he expressed strong disapproval,[1] that he established a colony as a refuge for those still faithful to Mother Church and that this became in a sense a rival to the Plymouth Plantation. In this connection attention is called to the fact that the wave of religious fervor that swept over the West of England at this period was entirely different from that which affected the East of England. Separation from the Church was not contemplated then in the West,

---

[1] *Planters Plea*, p. 35. His remarks here show that he was neither a Separatist nor Non-conformist. He declares that three-fourths of the men already settled in New England had "lived in a constant course of conformity unto our church government and orders," that Winthrop had been "every way regular and conformable in the whole course of his practise," and that "neither all nor the greatest part of the Ministers are unconformable."

the reformation of the Church from within was desired and attempted by clergymen of whom many were never obliged to relinquish their livings.

The association of Adventurers which the Rev. John White formed, known as the Dorchester Company, established a plantation on Cape Ann, a few men being left there as early as 1623 by the fleet sent out by the Western Merchants. It has been positively and persistently stated that this company "held of those of Plymouth," or that they "secured a permit for their settlement from the Plymouth colonists." [2] The facts refute definitely the assertion that the Dorchester Company was in any way dependent upon the Plymouth Plantation and show that it was always in opposition thereto.

The first inaccurate statement is based upon a paragraph in the first edition of Captain John Smith's *Generall Historie of Virginia:* "At Cape Ann there is a plantation beginning by the Dorchester Men, which hold of those of New Plymouth, who also by them have set up a Fishing Work." The *Historie* proper ends with the phrase "John Smith writ this with his own hand," but this paragraph is on a subsequent folio, not attached to the last gathering, evidently added to the book as it was passing through the press in 1623 [3]; it follows "Observations" by Captain Whitbourne and this independent sheet is headed: "The Present Estate of New Plymouth," and is signed "J. S." It contains information furnished to

[2] Osgood, *American Colonies,* I, p. 129.
[3] *Op. cit.,* p. 274. From the mistake of calling Captain Whitbourne "Charles" instead of Richard it is obvious that the last sheets had been carelessly prepared, no doubt due to the haste to get them ready at the last moment.

Smith by someone familiar with the affairs of that Plantation; quite possibly it came from James Sherley who knew of the application for the patent for Cape Ann and would have introduced the statement that the Dorchester men held of Plymouth for the express purpose of making out a case for his planters should the Sheffield grant be disputed.

It is asserted that this "Sheffield Patent" confirms the idea of the subordination to Plymouth, but that indenture granted permission to the Plymouth representatives to settle on a coast, over which Sheffield's jurisdiction is doubtful, provided the spot selected *was not already inhabited by English*. It is dated 1 January, 1623/4, but already in 1623 fourteen men had "inhabited" at Cape Ann and thirty-two more came there in the following spring. Bradford states that Winslow with the patent was delayed because the Western men had already taken up all the good seamen, so probably Winslow arrived after the Cape Ann contingent. He also mentions that they left but one man there that year to look after their fishing-gear. When the Plymouth planters with Miles Standish in command reached the spot in 1624, they found the shore occupied by a considerable body of men who disputed their claim. They must have recognized that the presence of Englishmen already inhabiting the territory barred their claim as they refused to fight either on the spot or in the law-courts, and tamely relinquished the much coveted fishing station to obtain which they had expended money on a "useless patent." Knowing their tenacity, it is difficult to believe they would have yielded had they been able to prove their claim. That the Dor-

chester men had been already established is evident from
the fact that Conant was present and acted as peace-
maker and he did not become governor of the plantation
until Tilly and Gardner had had charge of it for a year.

Moreover, if the Dorchester men held of New Plymouth,
there would have been ready means to enforce the Plymouth rights. But it is noticeable that Bradford no-
where states that the settlers at Cape Ann had obtained
permission from his colony. Had such been the case he
would most certainly have lamented the loss of the fishing station at Cape Ann in no measured terms. Another
fact tends to discredit the claim made for the Plymouth
overlordship. In a suit concerning salt left on an island
off Cape Ann, John White, as head of the Dorchester
Company, appears as the chief defendant, and in his evidence he refers to the equal culpability of the Plymouth
men in also removing salt, using phrases that indicate
that they were in no way associated with him.[4]

When the history of the Dorchester Company is considered, it is not surprising that that company was in
no way dependent upon the Plymouth colonists. It was
established as the outcome of John White's desire to provide religious instruction for "the fishermen and others
of our nation" upon the New England coast, and to provide a refuge to which churchmen could flee when no
longer able to comply with Laud's demands. This purpose appealed to a number of Puritans, a body to be distinguished from the Separatists—a distinction too often
blurred, and even ignored, chiefly because the religious
opinions of the later emigrants to Massachusetts Bay

[4] *Massachusetts Historical Society Proceedings,* 3rd. Series, Vol. 43.

very soon inclined towards Separatism, while the Plymouth colonists repudiated the designation "rigid Separatists," and by their convergence it became difficult to see where a line could be drawn between them. The divergence between the real Puritan and the Separatist lines of thought requires great emphasis as the difference in view point of the Puritans of Cape Ann and the Separatists of Plymouth provides a key to many puzzles which have baffled historians, especially when dealing with the half-way position of the Boston settlers.

When the plantation at Cape Ann showed promise and seemed likely to develop into a colony, John White and his friends invited the assistance of certain "religious and well-affected persons" who had, they heard, left Plymouth "out of dislike of the principles of rigid separation" held there.[5]

Lyford, "lately dismissed from Plymouth," was chosen to be their minister, Conant to be governor of their plantation, and Oldham to be manager of their trade; the very fact that these had a distaste for Plymouth religious opinions seems to have been a recommendation to the managers of the Dorchester Company, which is not surprising when it is recognized that that body counted among its one hundred and twenty members twenty-one Church of England clergymen of Puritan, but not Separatist, opinions, who retained their livings until after the Dorchester Company ceased to exist. In certain letters still

---

[5] Hubbard, *History of New England*, p. 105. Apparently while the Lyford trouble was in full swing Bradford wrote regarding "diversity about religion" among the objections of the discontented adventurers, "we know no such matters, for here was never any controversy or opposition either public or private (to our knowledge), since we came." *History*, ed. Ford, I, p. 362.

preserved, moreover, evidence is found confirming the view that the earlier Adventurers held the less advanced opinions mentioned; in the one of 17 April, 1629, written on behalf of the New England Company, reference is made to the suspicions entertained of the orthodoxy of Ralph Smith which proved to be correct, for eventually he found congenial spirits at New Plymouth. So too, when the charges made by the brothers Browne came to their notice the Company reproved the ministers for the expression of opinions which, if correctly reported, they strongly deprecated, nor did they view with approbation Endecott's injudicious action in expelling these two complaining patentees.

It cannot be denied when all the evidence is considered that the settlements made by the Dorchester men were undertaken for the purpose of assisting persons holding opinions almost diametrically opposed to those entertained by New Plymouth authorities and that, instead of being made under the auspices of the Pilgrim Fathers, they were established in direct opposition to those colonists and incurred their undying hatred.

III

THE NEW ENGLAND COMPANY

THE Dorchester Company, having, through misfortune, failed to accomplish its object, ceased to exist in 1626, and the plantations, servants and supplies were taken over by a few members of the Company who had not lost faith in the ultimate success of their purpose. In order to carry on the settlement, by this time transferred to Nahum Keike [Salem], they appealed to a group of Puritans, styled by them "the London merchants," for financial assistance. In order to obtain a patent for the land they had chosen it was necessary, in the view of the Council for New England, that application should be made by "gentlemen of blood," though on one occasion the privilege was extended to six Western merchants.[1] To meet this requirement John White obtained the cooperation of certain of his neighbours: Sir Henry Rosewell of Ford Abbey and of Lymington, Somerset; Thomas Southcote of Mohuns Ottery, Devon; Sir John Yonge of Colyton, Devon; Simon Whetcombe, a wealthy cloth-worker of Sherborne, and John Humfry of Dorchester, lately treasurer of the Dorchester Company.

Of John Endecott, the remaining patentee, nothing regarding his ancestry or occupation in England is defi-

[1] *Records of the Council for New England* (Deane), p. 13.

16

nitely known.[2] He appears to have been joined with the others for no other reason than that he was ready to emigrate for the purpose of taking charge of the plantation already established.

The Council for New England, being satisfied, a grant was made to these persons "and their associates." The contents of this grant can only be surmised for no exact copy is known to exist. The patent issued a year later purports to repeat its very words, but the accuracy of this is questionable because the docket attached shows that some additions were made, and Winthrop's claim that a phrase was abscinded, taken for what it is worth, suggests further alteration, but unfortunately we have no means of testing the truth of the matter.[3] The original grant was admittedly taken to New England, and although the Council for New England demanded its presentation before them, it was never produced; certain members of the Council suspected some irregularity in its wording or in the method by which it had been obtained,[4] and the fact that it has completely vanished lends colour to their charge.

By analogy with several others, it may be guessed that this grant was in the form of an indenture dealing with territory somewhat vaguely described, and that it con-

---

[2] Sir Roper Lethbridge tried to identify him with a John Endecott of Chagford but was unable to support his claim with satisfactory evidence. The idea that Endecott had been a surgeon while in England seems doubtful for the Plymouth doctor, Fuller, would hardly have been spared to go to Salem. The statement on this subject in my *Roger Conant and the North Shore Settlements* was inserted without my knowledge or sanction.

[3] See for these changes p. 79.

[4] *Records of the Council for New England* (Deane), p. 59.

tained provisos of a similar nature to those in the Peirce
and Sheffield grants. It was, as we know, made out to six
Patentees and their associates, so it may be assumed that
"letters of association" were taken out after definite limits
of the territory desired were set out and before application was made for the Charter, so that the term "associates" was here used indefinitely. There is no direct
evidence obtainable on these points, but when the methods
pursued by the Council, which are dealt with below, are
considered, the above surmise will seem likely to be correct.

We have now reached the period when a new company
came into existence, and its name and object are given at
the end of a letter written in its behalf: "The New
England Company for a Plantation in Massachusetts
Bay," [5] or as Higginson calls it "the Company of New
England." The earlier settlement, governed by Endecott,
was styled "London's Plantation in the Massachusetts
Bay in New England" in the official notice sent to him.[6]
What arrangement was made by this Company with the
Dorchester men who had possession of the Nahum Keike
plantation is not clear; Brackenbury says their rights
were bought out and Cradock, in a letter written several
years later, says: "to the best of my remembrance they
gave what they had there to go upon account of their
stock intended.[7] The vagueness of the transaction resulted in some unpleasantness in the early days of Salem.

The formation of the New England Company and the

---

[5] *Massachusetts Records,* I, p. 383.
[6] *Ibid.,* p. 361.
[7] *Winthrop Papers,* I, p. 125.

work accomplished, as far as that can be discovered, between 19 March, 1627/8, and 4 March, 1628/9, must next engage our attention. At the outset it is well to repeat that, as in the case of the Dorchester Company, their main object was religious; at the first opportunity they recorded that their enterprise was for "the propagation of the Gospel of Jesus Christ and the particular good of the several Adventurers," praying the Almighty "to grant prosperous and happie success, that the same may redound to his glorie."

The names of the first members of the New England Company, as it may be styled for the sake of brevity, are only to be found in the documents quoted by Felt from an unknown source;[8] the first, after its formal heading, "In the name of God, Amen," and the dating, "London, May, 1628," states that certain persons owe to "the general stock of the adventurers for plantation intended at Massachusetts Bay in New England in America," 2150^{li}, undertaken by these persons "by their several and general stock for the plantation," and the subscriptions named were "adventured in this Joint Stock" upon which they ask the blessing of the Almighty as above-mentioned.

The first two persons named subscribed 100^{li} and the rest 50^{li} each. Their occupations are not given but where they are known they are here placed in brackets.

Sir Richard Saltonstall, knt.
Mr. Isaac Johnson, Esqer.
Mr. Samuel Aldersey   [Haberdasher]
John Venn   [Captain and Merchant tailor]
Hugh Peter   [Minister]

[8] *Annals of Salem*, p. 508.

John Humfrey	[Gentleman]
Thomas Steevens	[Armourer]
George Harwood	[Haberdasher]
John Glover	[Gentleman]
Matthew Cradocke	[Skinner]
Simon Whetcombe	[Wool merchant]
Francis Webbe	
Increase Nowell	[Gentleman]
Mr. A. C.	
Richard Tuffneale	[Brewer]
Richard Perrie	[Merchant tailor]
Joseph Oldfield	[? Fishmonger]
John White	[Minister]
Joseph Caron	[Skinner]
Thomas Adams	[Woollen draper]
Richard Davis	[Vintner]
Abraham Palmer	[Merchant, ? Mercer]
William Darbie	[Mercer]
John Endecott	[? Surgeon]
Daniel Hodson	[Clothier]
Edward Foorde	[Leather seller]
Daniell Bullard	
Thomas Hewson	[Merchant]
Andrew Arnold	
Richard Bushrod	[Haberdasher]
Richard Young	[Cooper]
George Way	[Glover]
Richard Bellingham	[Gentleman, Lawyer]
Job Bradshawe ⎫ Joseph Bradshawe ⎭	[? Brewers]
Henry Durleye	[Gentleman]
Thomas Hutchins	
Charles Whitcholls	[Witchcote, Colonel]
George Foxcroft	[Merchant of Coleman Street]
William Crowther	[Haberdasher]
Nathaniel Manstreye	

The other list of money received from sundry Adventurers by George Harwood "Treasurer for the plantation of Massachusetts Bay" adds two names: Abrie, perhaps John Aubrey, a London Merchant, and John Smith, perhaps the famous Captain.

Among these forty-one Adventurers twenty-five are identified as men of business whose names are, hardly without exception, to be found elsewhere as subscribing to, or connected with, Puritan undertakings. A few have not been identified, and in the cases of Oldfield and the Bradshawes the occupations given are those of their fathers, which it is to be presumed they followed, so it can be said quite safely that the merchant class predominated. The "gentlemen" were mostly members of one of the Inns of Court.[9] Of these forty-one Adventurers, six had been members of the Dorchester Company. The total of the subscriptions in these two lists, counting the second instalment promised by John Smith, is 2940^{li}, very nearly touching the 3000^{li} usually estimated as sufficient to start such an enterprise.

It is impossible to state definitely what steps the Company took and what liabilities it incurred. A few things, however, may be inferred from the Records of the Massachusetts Bay Company, and a little light is obtainable from other sources.

The small body of Dorchester men who had agreed to

9 In his *True Relation* Higginson says the Company consisted of many worthy gentlemen of the city of London, Dorchester, and other places, aiming at the glory of God, the propagation of the Gospel of Christ, the conversion of the Indians and the enlargement of the King's Majesty's dominions in America." The omission of the names of "other places" is worth noting.

the transfer of their plantation to Nahum Keike had carried out their promise to send supplies and were so engaged when the new company came into existence. A considerable amount of material,—cattle, food and clothing,—were placed on board certain ships at Weymouth the very day after that on which the grant to Rosewell and his companions was executed, i.e. on 20 March, 1627/8, under a licence to "Simon Whetcombe and his associates," applied for undoubtedly by the Dorchester group several months earlier. A curious fact is that another vessel was freighted at Weymouth under the same licence in May and the Christian name of the master was Henry, but the entry is unfortunately rendered partly illegible by damp, so it is impossible to say whether this was the *Abigail*, Henry Gauden, Master, in which Endecott sailed about 20 June.[10] There would, of course, be nothing unusual in a delay of three weeks for the convenience of the Company or for that of Endecott.

Endecott's instructions were signed on 30 May, 1628, by fourteen of the Adventurers already named.[11] On his arrival at "London's Plantation," we learn from Brackenbury, he took over everything there on the ground that the "Massachusetts Pattentees," who had their court in Cornhill, had bought out the Dorchester Company's rights.[12] Endecott appears to have understood that the purchase covered all the property and services of every

[10] For particulars from the Weymouth Port Books see my forthcoming *John White, Founder of Massachusetts.*

[11] See Hutchinson, *History of Massachusetts,* I, p. 16. Unfortunately, the instructions themselves are lost.

[12] See his Deposition of 1680 given in *The Landing at Cape Ann,* p. 82. He may have used the title "Massachusetts Pattentees" as understood by the court addressed, though not in use in 1629.

person upon the Plantation; but certain "Old Planters" maintained that they, their services and their lands were not at the disposal of the Adventurers in London. They certainly possessed rights as pioneers, for they were already in New England when the management of the Dorchester Plantation was offered to them. Their claims seem to have been supported by John White, who was aware of the position they held. Eventually this was recognized and special grants were made to them.

From the entries on the first pages of the Massachusetts Records and documents published in the first volume, it may be inferred that the New England Company was in control of affairs when arrangements were begun for the emigration of several ministers and others in the spring of 1629, as we find that as early as November, 1628, steps were being taken to that end. This is evident from Cradock's letter of February, 1628/9,[13] in which he refers to a letter sent by Allerton in the previous November, probably taken over with those addressed to Plymouth and dated 18 November, and he repeats part of its contents. But even without this statement the despatch of instructions some time previous to those of February would naturally be inferred from Cradock's demand that Endecott should have ready sufficient cargo for the immediate return of the ships expected to sail on 20 March, for in a bare month Endecott could not have collected, besides the beaver, fish or timber accumulated in the ordinary course, sassafras, sarsaparilla, sumac, a ton-weight of silk grass, dye stuffs, and at least two or three hundred firkins of sturgeon, and also have prepared

13 *Massachusetts Records*, p. 385.

accommodation for between two and three hundred emigrants, one hundred cattle, and various supplies. The records also show that in February the *Talbot* and *Lyons Whelp* were being prepared for the voyage, that ordnance, clothing and other supplies were already in hand, that men skilled and unskilled were being engaged, and many other arrangements made before the Charter passed the Great Seal. It seems, therefore, a reasonable conclusion that those in control of the Company during 1628 were responsible for the preparation of the fleet which sailed at the opening of the season of 1629.[14]

But in the letters of 17 April and 28 May are some curious instructions which indicate a condition of affairs which it is difficult to understand. In the first of these Endecott is instructed "to give all good accommodation to our present Governor, Mr. Matthew Cradock, who, with some particular brethren of our Company, have deeply engaged themselves in their private adventures in these ships and those to come and as we hold these men that thus deeply adventure in their private to be (under God) special instruments for the advancing & strengthening of our plantation, which is done by them without any charge to the Company's general stock, wherein, notwithstanding, they are as deep or deeper engaged than any other, so being contented to be debarred from all private trading in furs for three years, we do hold it very requisite in all other their desires to give them all accommo-

---

[14] It is suggested that these items were copied from the minute book of the New England Company because they had reference to the fleet which sailed after the Massachusetts Bay Company was incorporated; the irregularity of the entries and the absence of definite dates seems to bear this out.

dation and furtherance that reasonably may be propounded by them or any of them, their good beginnings in the infancy of our plantation worthily deserving of us all favour and furtherance." [15]

Cradock and his partners, who had done so much in the infancy of "London's Plantation," must have been members of the New England Company, perhaps to be identified with the "Old Adventurers." Their undertakings were considerable, and the arrangement made for the division of expenses, etc., between them and the Company was remarkable.

On 3 March, 1628/9, the day before the sealing of the Charter, Samuel Sharpe, Cradock's agent, agreed with the Company to oversee their ordnance, and he was "also entertained to oversee the [servants] and implements of certain particular men of the company." On the day the Assistants took the oath, 23 March, two coopers were engaged, and "the company hath agreed that they shall go half at the charge of Mr. Governor the one half, and at the charge of the company the other half." On 11 March, Claydon, a carpenter and wheelwright, had proposed to go out with his family, including his brother Barnaby, also a wheelwright, he paying part cost and working out the balance by instructing servants of the Company. A third wheelwright was afterwards engaged whose expenses and labours were to be shared in thirds by Cradock and the Company; but a simpler arrangement was made by assigning Barnaby Claydon to serve Sharpe, Cradock's agent. In May, nine fishermen were sent out,

[15] *Massachusetts Records*, I, p. 391. Modern spelling has been adopted here and elsewhere.

three of these were Cradock's and six were sent out by
the Dorchester men, and the combined costs were to be
shared proportionably by the Company and Cradock and
his partners, who were also to have a third interest in the
shallops built and the benefits derived from the labours
of the fishermen, either in fishing or as seamen, except
when they were engaged in the beaver trade, a Government monopoly, for which a different arrangement was
made.

The question of the cattle is of special interest. The
letter of November, 1628, mentions the intention of sending one hundred cattle, but the Lord Treasurer's warrant
sanctioned the despatch of as many as one hundred and
forty; the letter of 28 May states that all the cattle except three mares from Leicester, had been provided by
Cradock, but in this instance there was to be an equal
division between him and the Company.[16]

Three ships, the *Mayflower* of Yarmouth, the *Four Sisters* of London, and the *Pilgrim* of the same,[17] were also
shared equally and so were the freighting charges, the
wages and victuals of the men, as well as the victuals of
the passengers, a special reference being made to the Governor and his partners and "their private stock." The
salt sent in the ships and the "fishing to be returned in
them" were similarly apportioned, while the surplus
victuals after their arrival were to be divided between
Endecott and Cradock's agent, Sharpe. "All provision
for the fishing at sea is here equally borne in halves; so

---

[16] Francis Higginson, *A True Relation*, says that the *George* carried 12 mares, 30 kyne, and some goats, and the *Four Sisters* carried many cattle.

[17] Was the *George* substituted for the *Pilgrim*?

are all the provisions of shipping of all the cattle in the
three ships; and accordingly we desire the deals and casks
may be equally divided there."

Cradock took particular interest in shipbuilding and
early established a shipyard on the Mystic. A week after
the swearing in of the Assistants, 30 March, 1629, Robert
Molton, a shipwright, was paid 10^{li}, apparently earnest-
money. On 2 April, it was agreed that he and two or
three men were to go to New England, Mr. Governor to
bear two-thirds of their charges. Altogether six shipwrights had been sent out when on 28 May a seventh,
George Farre, sailed; his charges were to be shared in
thirds by the two parties before-named. The material
for shipbuilding, pitch, tar, oakum, etc., sent in the *Four
Sisters*, were to be similarly shared. A storehouse was
to be built and an inventory made of the old implements
and of those added and of all the shipbuilding material
sent or hereafter sent, and such inventory was to be forwarded to the Company "to the end we may here examine
and find out that the Company may be charged with their
two-thirds part of the charge and no more" and "the
Governor likewise." The shipwrights were to be kept at
work together and an equal number of the Company's
servants and of the Governor's might be employed to help
them when required. As regards the results of their
labour, both parties were to be accommodated for the
present occasions but when three shallops had been completed two were to go by lot to the Company and one to
Cradock's party, but with a proviso that some equitable
arrangement might be reached with Sharpe if Endecott
thought fit. The Company remarks that the Governor

has engaged himself beyond all expectation in this business, not only in "his particular" but "by great sums disbursed in the general to supply the wants hereof" so that special pains were to be taken that the charges should be borne indifferently and proportionably; but the management of this was left to Endecott's discretion, "desiring and heartily praying that love and amity may be continued without any heart-burnings." As the Governor has done so much, Endecott is to endeavour "to give all furtherance and friendly accommodation to his agents and servants there, not doubting but you will find them likewise ready to accommodate the Company in what they may, the Company standing in need of their help."

It will be seen from this that the shipbuilders were all to work together and it is known that Cradock had a shipyard on the Mystic. The firstfruit of their labours may have been the "Blessing of the Bay," which Winthrop, under 4 July, 1631, says the governor built at Mystic. Fully occupied as he was since his arrival and the Ten Hills estate not yet having been granted to him, it is hard to believe that Winthrop established a rival shipyard, so we can only conclude that he meant the bark was built for him. No reference is elsewhere made to his shipbuilding.

It is difficult to reach any satisfactory conclusion concerning the undertakings of Cradock and his partners. Is it possible that a body of the earlier adventurers, those who had done so much in the infancy of the plantation, retained control of an enterprise already fairly well advanced when the Massachusetts Bay Company was incorporated, and that the new Company, disapproving of this *imperium in imperio,* which was likely to cause friction, found it advisable to come to some agreement to get control of it by obtaining a two-thirds interest in the business? Did Cradock's party include all, or nearly all, the members of the New England Company? and was the arrangement made as compensation for their rights? or did the corporation buy out two-thirds of their interest, or, alternatively, allow them a one-third share in the new enterprise? The latter suggestion seems the more reasonable in view of the claims made by the persons styled "the Old Adventurers."

In spite of the Company's instructions "to give all furtherance and friendly accommodation" to Cradock's servants, friction did develop, at all events as soon as the government was transferred to New England, if not earlier. Immediately after Winthrop arrived, the first coroner's jury sat upon the body of Bratcher, killed on Cradock's plantation. Fox, a servant of Cradock, suggested that the verdict was obtained by bribery, and, for "traducing the Court," he was whipped. Ratcliffe, another servant, for "malicious speeches against the government and church of Salem," was fined, whipped, and had his ears cut off.[18] Greater offences were, on other occasions, punished by fines or banishment, and, as far as the evidence goes, this case would have been met by sending Rat-

[18] This punishment does not appear to have been inflicted in any other early case in the colony. C. F. Adams, *Three Episodes,* p. 262, compares this sentence with Prynne's, so vehemently denounced by all Puritans, and on p. 349 comments on the severe punishments inflicted by the mere dictum of a board of magistrates. Thomas Morton says Ratcliffe was a churchman and that Sir Christopher Gardiner persuaded Winthrop to reduce a more severe sentence to that inflicted.

cliffe back under arrest to his master. It is not surprising to learn that Cradock considered himself much abused by the authorities in New England. Humfry, in 1630, tells us that Cradock was very much afflicted by the unkindness shown by all the magistrates in consenting to the action taken against him. He declared that when it was found necessary to reduce the number on the plantation they reckoned his servants the worst, but instead of sending them back, they were advised to defer so doing until after his, Cradock's, ships returned, lest seeing his servants decreased and "his particular" not needing such large supplies, the plantation would lose the benefit of what he might send. He complained that the magistrates cared not what burdens they laid on him or what injury they did him. Humfry reminds them that of all interested in the plantation none retains so lively affection for them, nor is able to do them such service with the State, or, being provoked, so much injury.[19]

In 1636, Cradock exclaims "For my particular I profess unfeignedly to my best knowledge I am out of purse for the general Company betwixt 3 and 400^{li}, and have been so for many years, what recompense I shall have I know not, and it is not fit that any man should bear a burden the general body of the Company ought to bear. . . . As I once delivered at a full board at Council table so I have great cause to acknowledge God's goodness and mercy to me in enabling me to undergo what I have and do suffer by New England, and as I spake then openly so I profess sincerely if my heart deceive me not, I joy more in the expectation of that good shall come to others

[19] *Winthrop Papers*, I, p. 12.

there when I shall be dead and gone, than I grieve for my own losses, though they have been very heavy and great, seeing God hath enabled me to bear them." [20] Yet with touching nobility, he adds, "I understand there is voluntary contribution towards a College in Cambridge, which I must confess is a worthy work. I pray, worshipful sir, be pleased to move the Court to clear that debt due to me by the Country, out of which money I am content and do freely give fifty pounds to the said College and for the advancement thereof." [21] No record exists that Harvard College ever received this gift.

[20] The claim by his widow for over 679li, made more than once, was repudiated by the Massachusetts Court because the money that had been paid or expended concerned "only particular persons, or company of merchants, or undertakers, and not the government now established." 15 October, 1650. *Massachusetts Records*, III, p. 213.
[21] *Winthrop Papers*, I, pp. 125, 129.

IV

THE WORK OF THE NEW ENGLAND COMPANY

OTHER arrangements made for the fleet which sailed in the spring of 1629 are equally interesting. In the letter of 16 February Endecott was informed that "It is fully resolved, by God's assistance, to send over two ministers at least with the ships now intended to be sent thither; but for Mr. Peters, he is now in Holland from whence his return hither I hold to be uncertain. Those we send shall be by the approbation of Mr. White of Dorchester and Mr. Davenport." [1] On 17 April they mention those selected: Skelton, because he was known to Endecott; Higginson, "a grave man;" Bright, trained up by Mr. Davenport, and Ralph Smith, whose suitability was questioned. Their selection and subsequent events throw an interesting light upon the development of religious opinion in the colony.

Attention has already been drawn to the fact that the West Country men who began the settlement on the North Shore were Puritans and not Separatists, while those who came over in 1630, mostly from the East Coast, had been much affected by the Separatist opinions so widely held

---

[1] *Massachusetts Records,* I, 385. Johnson, writing to Winthrop, 17 December, 1629, says: "Touching Mr. Peters your caution is good but I hope we shall give you content, that his place will not be unsupplied, nor his coming over offensive nor dangerous." *Winthrop Papers,* I, p. 31.

in that district. At the time of the migration in May, 1629, both John White and John Davenport were still clergymen of the Church of England who had not attracted the unpleasant attentions of the ecclesiastical authorities. It was not until 1633 that Davenport resigned the living of St. Stephen's, Coleman Street, and Bright had been his disciple. The latter was the first minister to enter into an agreement with the Company to go to New England.

Higginson had been suggested by Increase Nowell, who was in sympathy with the East Anglians, and Skelton, from Sempringham, is said to have been looking towards Separatism. Ralph Smith went out on his own account, not being one accepted by the scrutineers, for he "desired passage in our ships, which was granted him before we understood of his difference of judgment in some things from our ministers," but they hoped they would not "offend in charity to fear the worst that may grow from their different judgments" as they had a good opinion of his honesty, but if he was not conformable to their government he was not to be allowed to remain on the plantation.[2] It is therefore clear that those at this time in charge of the Company's affairs held Puritan rather than Separatist opinions.

Soon after landing, Bright went with the party sent to occupy land claimed by Oldham, to Charlestown, where he found a congenial spirit in Blackstone, a Church of England clergyman. He took the earliest opportunity to return to England because he was not in sympathy with the tendency to Separation that was beginning to develope

[2] *Ibid.*, p. 390.

in the colony. Higginson had already been forced to relinquish his living; Skelton had apparently advanced
much further on the road to Separatism, and Endecott,
who had sat under him before leaving England, was led
nearer to the opinions of the Plymouth planters by their
physician, Samuel Fuller. But Ralph Smith was much
more in sympathy with the Plymouth Separatists than
even with these two ministers and eventually found the
settlers in that colony more to his taste, so joined them.

It is not necessary here to dwell upon the well-known
action of Higginson and Skelton, backed by Endecott, in
establishing a church government which could scarcely
be distinguished from that of the Plymouth Separatists.
But attention should be drawn to the fact that when
rumours of the form of church government set up at
Salem reached the Company in England they took the
matter under advisement. While they hoped there was
no foundation for the charge, they wrote both to the
ministers and the Governor deprecating the adoption of
rash innovations in civil and ecclesiastical government; if
the rumour was true they called upon the ministers to
repent their miscarriage and thus remove the dangers in
which such action might involve the Company, and Endecott was seriously reproved for his, seemingly, rash and
undigested councils put suddenly in execution.[3]

The charges were brought by the brothers Browne,
against whom Endecott, to put it mildly, had acted
rashly. The Brownes, probably friends of, and holding
the same opinions as, John White of Dorchester, remained faithful to the Church of England. They had

[3] *Ibid.,* pp. 407, 408.

emigrated at their own expense and therefore by the payment of only 5^{li} they were accounted Adventurers. The
Company in its letter had highly commended them to
Endecott; they were both named as Associates of the
Rosewell Patentees and John Browne was sworn an Assistant; both brothers were appointed members of Endecott's Council and as such were at liberty to express their
opinions. Being devout Churchmen, they naturally disapproved of the action of the ministers, and therefore
assembled other settlers who agreed with them, probably
all the Old Planters among them, and read the service
from the Book of Common Prayer. Endecott, angry at
such proceedings, haled them before the Council, which
then consisted of the two ministers and the three members
he had co-opted,[4] who would have supported him, while
the minister Bright, if he chanced to be in Salem, perhaps
Samuel Sharpe, Cradock's agent, and the two representatives of the Old Planters most probably supported the
Brownes. Before these fellow-councillors, some of whom
combined the offices of accusers, jury and judges, they
were arraigned, and for objecting to ecclesiastical
changes not yet authorized by any higher authority, they
were condemned, deprived of their possessions at a low
valuation, shipped home as if under arrest, and charged
for their passage. It had not yet been made a legal
offence to read the Prayer Book, and such action was
repugnant to the laws of England, so, to compass his purpose, Endecott charged them with being disturbers of the
peace, and as such he claimed that he had authority to
expel them from the plantation, adding that "New

4 Who these three were is not known.

England was no place for such as they." It was an outrageous proceeding and it was ridiculous to assert that the action of those who objected to the introduction of a new form of religious worship, devised by two ministers whose action was endorsed by only thirty out of more than two hundred settlers, would endanger the peace of the colony. Endecott evidently intended to stretch his authority to the utmost in order to force the acceptance of this change even if such a course were repugnant to the laws of England.

The Brownes' [5] case was heard by the Company, and they so far substantiated their claims that their damage and loss were admitted, the sum entered for an undervaluation of their goods was paid subject to revision if Governor Winthrop found the "praisers" estimate correct. In order to make a "final end" of the business, the other matters were referred to a committee, provided the Brownes agreed to accept their arbitration. By this acceptance of their liability the Company admitted the malfeasance of their servant, and they even despatched a letter of reproof though reserving their condemnation of the ill-digested action until they heard the defence put forward by Endecott and the ministers.

[5] Osgood, *American Colonies,* I, p. 204, states, inaccurately, that the Brownes objected to the doings of the ministers on the outward voyage, but it was after the establishment of the Salem church by Higginson and Skelton that they gathered a company together. He claims that this assembly "establishes the fact that it [the Prayer Book] was not used in the religious meetings at Salem." It points rather to its use prior to the arrival of Higginson; there is no question that it was not used after the church was established. He says "the damage which they claimed to have suffered was referred to a committee, but what decision was reached we are not told."

That actual financial loss had been incurred by the Brownes is obvious,[6] and compensation was merely an act of justice, so that any suggestion that they consented to suppress the expression of their religious opinions because they were bribed is a perversion of the truth.

From all that has been said it is evident that the religious opinions prevailing among those who managed the earlier enterprises were distinctly Puritan as opposed to Separatist—the clergy appointed to select ministers had sent out Bright, a faithful churchman, and had disapproved of Smith, the Separatist; the Brownes, Associates, Assistants and Councillors, found enough churchmen among the settlers desiring to hear the Church services to enrage Endecott, while the persecution of the two churchmen was repudiated by the Company at home. It was only on the introduction of the East Anglian element, which tended towards Separation, though not openly shown, that a change of orientation took place, with the result that under such influences the emigrants of 1630, after their arrival, accepted a form of worship and church government allied to that of Plymouth and so distasteful to the Puritans at home that even so old and firm a friend of the enterprise as John White remonstrated with Winthrop, and other prominent Puritans in England carried on a bitter controversy with the leaders at Boston.

[6] They had relinquished their business interests; had paid their passage out; had been deprived of the land they had begun to improve and the profits from their crops planted; had had their goods sold at a cheap rate; had been charged for their journey home undertaken against their will, and even for freight on their goods; and a box of evidences, required in the presentation of their case, had been detained as security for payment.

Considering all these circumstances, the much disputed authorship of the "Humble Request" assumes an unrecognized aspect. It shows signs of having been prepared by one holding Puritan opinions who had no intention of leaving "dear Mother Church," and its authorship was rightly attributed to John White of Dorchester by Hubbard. It was not signed until the very eve of the actual sailing of the *Arbella*, and, taken in conjunction with the fears expressed in the letters to Endecott and the ministers that the displeasure of the authorities might be incurred, it may be surmised that the signers were pressed to accept the form of words contained in the document. Some of them had not as yet expressed their own views openly, though there can be no question that Phillips' views did not coincide with those expressed in the document he signed. The signers possibly accepted the position maintained later by the Separatists, that *they* held to the true "Mother Church," while the others had separated themselves from that body, so, without violation of conscience, for politic reasons they set their names to the document offered.[7]

[7] The delay in signing is significant; the *Arbella* had been expected to sail daily for some time, but it was only when within a few hours of actual departure that the signatures were affixed.

V

THE EAST COAST ELEMENT

AFTER this digression let us revert to the consideration of the situation at the time of the change of control in the affairs of the Company, or rather to an even earlier period, when a larger enterprise than that of the New England Company was being considered and, in order to allow of its execution, application was made for a Charter.

White, in his *Planters Plea*, carries on the story after Endecott's arrival in New England and the increase of the company due to the knowledge of his prosperous journey as well as the despatch of more servants and rother beasts. "By this time the often agitation of this affair in sundry parts of the kingdom, the good report of Captain Endecott's Government and the increase of the colony began to awaken the Spirits of some persons of competent estates, not formerly engaged, considering that they live either without useful employment at home, and might be more serviceable in assisting the planting of a Colony in New England, took at last a resolution to unite themselves for the prosecution of that work." [1]

It is quite clear from this statement that it was not until Endecott's success was known that these men of competent estates *began* to consider the question of emigrating

[1] *Op. cit.*, p. 43.

in person, and White can refer to none other than the East Country men, such as Winthrop, Dudley, and others whose names first appear in the Records late in 1629. That they were stirring in the matter is evident from the following curious entry under 2 March, 1628/9: "It being propounded by Mr. Coney, in the behalf of the Boston men (whereof divers had promised, though not in our books under written, to adventure 400^{li} for the joint stock), that now their desire was that 10 persons of them might underwrite 25^{li} a man to the joint stock, they withal promising with these ships to adventure in their particular above 250^{li} more, and to provide able men to send over for managing the business, which, though it be prejudicial to the general stock by the abatement of so much money thereout, yet appearing really to conduce to the good of the Plantation, which is most desired, it was condescended unto." [2]

From this it is evident that the "Boston men," who may be identified with those connected with the Earl of Lincoln's family or with John Cotton's Church, had not become fully fledged Adventurers before this date. We know from the letter of 17 April that Saltonstall and Johnson sent over servants in the spring of 1629, but these were the only ones of this group who were, as far as we know, members of the Company any length of time before that date. In view of this fact we are astounded by the statement made by Dudley in these words: "about the year 1627 some friends being together in Lincolnshire, fell into some discourse about New England and the planting of the

---

[2] *Massachusetts Records,* I, p. 28. Perhaps it was the widow of the above agent, Margaret Coney of Boston, Lincs., who left a legacy to her brother John Cotton and her sister Cotton in 1652. [*P. C. C. Brent,* 88.]

Gospel there; and after some deliberation, we imparted our reasons by letters and messages to some in London and the west country where it was likewise deliberately thought upon, and at length with often negotiation so ripened that in the year 1628 we procured a patent." He proceeds to claim that "we" sent out Endecott to begin a plantation with those "we" had sent from Dorchester.

It can only be described as preposterous that he should claim that those in Lincolnshire had introduced the religious element, ascribing the honour and glory to his friends. It has been repeatedly pointed out that from the very beginning of the North Shore settlements the object entertained was the spread of religion; the Dorchester Company, composed so largely of Puritan clergy, was formed in order that ministers might go out to care for the souls of the fishermen and others of our nation; the New England Company announced at the outset in the most solemn manner that their enterprise was for "the propagation of the Gospel of Jesus Christ." Yet these upstart Lincolnshire men claimed all the glory attaching to the task begun at least four years earlier, and it was not until after the favourable report of Endecott that their spirits *began* to be awakened to the consideration of personal emigration to a colony already established and promising to prove successful. Upon this unwarranted assumption made by Dudley a writer of such standing as H. L. Osgood has referred to the Dorchester Company's plantation as only a "fishing enterprise"! [3]

---

[3] Osgood, *American Colonies,* I, p. 143, speaks slightingly of the "Dorchester fishermen"; Dorchester is not a seaport. He should have said, if need were, "fishermen sent by the Dorchester Company, that body being composed of clergy and merchants."

Inaccurate statements concerning that enterprise and the pioneers that established it have been made either by the later emigrants themselves or by those who have compiled accounts of the colony. One wonders whether these are due to ignorance or to a desire to praise the persons obtaining power in 1630 deliberately at the expense of the pioneers who laid the foundations upon which the later comers raised the superstructure.

Another puzzling point is the objection raised by the Old Planters concerning the transfer of their possessions and services to the new company. Their protest, forwarded by Endecott, was under consideration at the very moment the patent of the Bay Company was issued. The danger that these experienced pioneers would join Oldham's settlement led to conciliatory measures being sanctioned. The Old Planters, already in New England before the Nahum Keike plantation was started, had not gone out at the cost of the Company, and this, with their services, should have entitled them to the privileges conferred upon the Brownes as above mentioned, and doubtless they claimed this in their controversy with Endecott. If, then, they were in the position of Adventurers, it is difficult to understand why the Company wrote, in order that they and the world might know they had no intention of making the Old Planters slaves, as some of them declared the Patent made them, "we are content they shall be partakers of such privileges as we, from his Majesty's especial grace, with great cost, favour of personages of note, and much labour have obtained; and that they shall be incorporated into this Society, and enjoy not only those lands which formerly they have manured, but such a further proportion" as Endecott and his Council thought fit, and besides, "it is still our purpose that they should have some benefit by the Common Stock, as was by your first commission directed and appointed" at even a lower rate than 30 per cent. as had been proposed.[4] To obtain these advantages they must be such as would agree to reside and be well behaved. All this was granted as a favour. If they were already in the position of Adventurers, and if those of the New England Company automatically became members of the Bay Company, such privileges would have been theirs of right; if they were not counted as Adventurers, then these favours were granted to outsiders without apparent authority of the Charter.

[4] This paragraph reads as if it really had been intended not only to deny them a share in the provisions &c. sent, but to deprive them of the hard-earned profits of their labours, treating them indeed as serfs *adscripta gleba*.

VI

THE GORGES POSITION

IT has been difficult, even by means of analogy and inference, to arrive at an idea of the work accomplished
or undertaken by the New England Company between the
date of Endecott's departure and the date when the Patent
was obtained, and it is almost impossible, even by the same
processes, to arrive at any satisfactory conclusion concerning the events leading up to and connected with the
application for the Letters Patent and the way in which
the funds and business of the New England Company
passed to the newly incorporated body, except vaguely,
that some financial arrangement was made by which the
property of the Old Adventurers passed to the New ones
or became amalgamated by giving to the Old ones "fully
paid up shares," in modern parlance, in the new Company.
But the reasons for seeking a patent and the means employed to obtain it are so important that a careful study
of the subject and a co-ordination of the information we
do possess must be undertaken in order to form an opinion
on the transaction.

White indicates that the men of competent estate intended to emigrate in person, and from subsequent events
we know they had then, or developed later, an ambitious
scheme. How far this was formulated before application

was made for the patent or whether they had then only vague dreams that expanded and materialized after it was obtained, it is difficult to say with any great degree of certainty.

It may, however, be safely assumed that these gentlemen-emigrants had in mind from the outset an enterprise of much greater importance than that begun at London's Plantation, one requiring a larger amount of territory than was covered by the "Rosewell Grant." To that end, when applying for their letters of association, they appear to have asked the Council for New England to enlarge their bounds. At the time of their application the president of the Council was the Earl of Warwick who was in sympathy with them and inclined to further their aims; as it proved, he was also in a position to do pretty much as he pleased owing to the easy-going methods of his fellow-councillors.

Already, as early as 31 May, 1622, the Council had issued a grant of land of considerable extent on the shores of Massachusetts Bay to the Earl of Warwick, Lord Gorges, Sir Robert Mansell, and Sir Ferdinando Gorges, and, from statements made by the last-named, we know that on this territory Robert Gorges undertook to make a settlement, probably obtaining from the Patentees a roving commission, like that of Peirce, or rather that made by Lord Sheffield, authorizing him to select a portion of the land covered, establish a settlement and, when he had delimited the part desired, a patent would be issued to him. He proceeded to send out factors and servants to establish his settlement and, on 27 November, 1622, we find, he paid 160^{li} to the Council for a Patent which was issued on 30 December, following; this covered a district ten miles by thirty "upon the north-east side of the Bay called or known by the name of Massachusetts." Upon this land his plantation was begun.

Owing to complaints of abuses committed by fishermen and other interlopers, the Council for New England in 1623 appointed Robert Gorges their lieutenant, or governor, "to regulate the state of their affairs and those abuses," selecting him "because he was one of the company and interested in a portion of the land with other patentees [Warwick and his associates] in the Bay of Massachusetts."

When Robert Gorges reached New England in August, 1623, he made Wessaguscus his headquarters; it was conveniently situated for the administrative purposes of a "governor," and some buildings erected for Weston's colony remained there. According to Bradford he was "going to the eastward" to find Weston when he was forced into Plymouth Harbour for shelter, and there he found the delinquent with whom he dealt for his evil conduct, especially for the transport of arms, licenced for New England, but sold to the Spaniards, a matter which had made Sir Ferdinando "suffer a shrowd check." [1]

During his stay in New England Gorges must have visited his plantation "at the bottom of the Bay," where the 1630 emigrants found several of his servants "in charge and custody of his settled plantation," of which

[1] Bradford, *History*, ed. Ford, II, p. 331. Writers have frequently scoffed at the appointment of Robert Gorges as Governor of Massachusetts with a large staff, but it is clear that he effectually dealt with the particular business assigned to him on this occasion by the Council; he was easily discouraged, and his training had not fitted him for his task.

he had in person "taken an absolute seizure and actual
possession," while others had scattered or had stayed at
Wessaguscus; among the former were:—Blackstone and
Jeffries, who were to give seisin afterwards to Oldham
and Dorrell, Maverick, Walford, Thomson and Burslem
—a sufficient number to prove his claim by actual occupation of the land—a claim that was the stronger because
the grantee had visited it in person, as so few did in the
early days.

The documents relating to the affairs of the Council
for New England still in existence are very few and cannot have been originally as plentiful as we would expect
of a company of its kind—no register of grants was kept,
as will be seen from the request to Warwick mentioned
below; business affairs had been allowed to become very
confused, and Warwick himself fell under the suspicion
of his fellow-councillors. Concerning the situation Mr.
Deane writes: "There seems at this time to have arisen
a serious misunderstanding or quarrel between the Council and their President, the Earl of Warwick. It first
appears at a meeting held June 29, 1632. The President
was not present at this meeting, though it was held, as
the meetings had been held for some time past, at 'Warwick House.' An order was adopted 'that the Earl of
Warwick should be entreated to direct a course for finding out what patents have been granted for New
England.' At the same meeting the clerk was sent to the
Earl for the Council's great seal, which was in his lordship's keeping, and word came back that he would send
it when his man came in. It was ordered that the future
meetings of the Council be held in the house of Captain

Mason in Fenchurch Street. But the seal was not sent,
and two more formal requests were made during the next
six months." [2] It may be added that on one of these latter occasions the Lord Great Chamberlain was instructed
to insist upon its delivery and Gorges promised to urge
the Marshal to use his influence to obtain the seal as it
was required for the patents that were to be issued.[3]

Unfortunately, no minutes of the Council have been
preserved for 1628/9, in which year such important events
connected with the Bay Company were taking place, but
information from other sources, and the course of subsequent events, may provide a reasonable conjecture.

When application was made for an extension of territory by the holders of the Rosewell grant, Warwick
appears to have contemplated giving the petitioners a
portion of the land, if not the whole, contained in the
grant of 1622 made to him and his associates, for his
first step was to ask the consent of one, if not all, of his
associates to the transfer of the land to the Company
now applying. Gorges, we know, consented "so far forth
as it might not be prejudicial to my son Robert Gorges'
interests," probably expecting that a reservation would
be made of his plantation. It may be that the other

---

[2] *History of America* [Justin Winsor], III, p. 309. A. P. Newton [*Puritan Colonization*, p. 83] questions Warwick's right as President of the Council to make grants of territory, such right being
vested in the Council; he calls attention to the informality of his
grant to Connecticut, though it was really a regrant; so was the
above—a regrant of land granted to him and others. Newton comments that, *with the exception of Herbert Pelham,* all named in the
Connecticut grant were "intimately interested in the Puritan emigration to Massachusetts." Pelham was a subscriber to the Bay
Company in 1629 and emigrated himself in 1638.

[3] *Records of the Council for New England* [Deane], p. 63.

patentees gave their unqualified assent. What appears to have happened is that Warwick, either ignoring Gorges' proviso or considering the consent of the majority sufficient to allow him to override it, handed over the actual patent, made in his and their names, to the petitioners; quite possibly he endorsed it properly as President of the Council and sealed it with the Council's seal. In confirmation of such a suggestion we have the entry in the Records of Massachusetts under 29 September, 1629,— as it happens the very day the transfer of the patent was to be considered: "It is thought fit and ordered that the Secretary shall write out a copy of the former grant to the Earl of Warwick and others, which was *by them resigned to this company* to be presented to his Lordship, as he having desired the same." [4]

What Gorges wrote concerning this whole business is in consonance with such a supposition. After reference to those who despaired of the reformation of the Church of England, he writes: "Some of the discreeter sort . . . made use of their friends, to procure from the Council for the Affairs of New England to settle a colony within their limits; to which it pleased the thrice-honoured Lord of Warwick to write to me, then at Plymouth, to condescend that a patent might be granted to such as then sued for it. Whereupon I gave my approbation so far forth as it might not be prejudicial to my son Robert Gorges' interests, whereof he had a Patent under the seal of the Council. Hereupon there was a grant passed as was thought reasonable; but the same was afterwards enlarged by his Majesty, and confirmed under the great

[4] *Massachusetts Records,* I, p. 53.

seal of England." [5] Furthermore, in the preamble to the
proposed surrender of the Council's charter in 1635, he
says that "certain that desired a Patent of some lands
in the Massachusetts Bay to plant upon, who presenting
the names of honest and religious men easily obtained
their first desires, but those being once gotten they used
other means to advance themselves a step far beyond their
first proportions to a second grant surreptitiously gotten
of other lands also, justly passed unto Captain Gorges
long before, who being made Governor in those parts went
in person and took an absolute seizure and actual possession of that country by a settled plantation he made
in the Massachusetts Bay, which afterwards he left to the
charge and custody of his servants and certain other
undertakers and tenants belonging unto some of us, who
were all thrust out by these intruders that had exorbi-
tantly bounded their grant from east to west through all
that main [land] from sea to sea, being near about 3000
miles in length, withal riding over the heads of all those
Lords and others that had their portions assigned unto
them in his Majesty's presence and with his Highness'
approbation, by lot upon the South Coast from east to
west some 80 or 100 leagues long. But herewith not yet
content they laboured and obtained unknown to us, a confirmation of all this from his Majesty and unwitting thereof, by which means they did not only enlarge their first
extents to the west limits spoken of, but wholly excluded
themselves from the public government of the Council authorized for those affairs, and made themselves a free
people." [6]

[5] *Brief Narration,* p. 40.
[6] *Records of the Council for New England* [Deane], p. 76.

That there was ground for these insinuations or
charges is probable, and we may surmise that when they
had in hand the Rosewell grant, obtained by "honest and
religious men" and the "second [Warwick] grant surreptitiously gotten," both were presented to the proper authorities with an application for a charter covering the
entire territory of the two. The documents properly executed and sealed would have been considered by those
whose business it was to prepare the Letters Patent per-
fectly in order, so without hesitation the charter would
have been drawn up; nor, after "the great costs, favour
of personages of note and much labour" had done their
work, would the higher authorities have objected to the
execution of the Letters Patent, which, of course, would
have been superior to the Council's grant, not only "enabling them to enlarge their territory, but withal riding over
the heads of all others . . . so that they made themselves"
a people free from the Council's interference.

Sir Ferdinando was probably at first not aware of
what had taken place, but complaints from the settlers
on Robert's land of the treatment meted out to them by
Winthrop's party would have brought the high-handed
proceedings of the newcomers to his notice, so, enquiry
disclosing their claims, he approached Humfry. The
latter wrote on 9 December, 1630, to Isaac Johnson that
Sir Ferdinando "who from very high matters has come
to this to desire that his people and planters (by virtue
of his son's patent) may live quietly and uninjured by
us; that Jeffries is a bad man, he basely flings out in his
letter to him, which Sir Ferdinando showed me, handle
him wisely and by no means exasperate such spirits.
Though Sir Ferdinando neither will nor can do us much

good, yet he or any may have care to do us hurt. I assured him of your care to right his people in any injury they had or should sustain and there was an end of the matter for the time." [7]

The "very high matters" may well have been connected with Robert Gorges' claim, and of this Humfry seems to have anticipated they would hear more.

But the true state of the case must have become known to Gorges before 26 June, 1633, when Humfry appeared before the Council for New England to complain that his Company's ships and passengers had been prevented from sailing unless holding a licence from the Council for New England, though they had both their grant and the King's confirmation of the privilege to transport them. "Hereupon some of the Council desired to see the Patent which they had obtained from the President and Council, because, as they alleged, it prejudiced former grants. Mr. Humfry answered that the *said* Patent was now in New England, and that they had ofttimes written for it to be sent hither, but as yet they had not received it. Hereupon the President and Council prayed him to be at their next meeting . . . and to bring with him Mr. Matthew Cradock, and such others as he should think fit, and then they should receive the President and Council's further answer unto his proposition." [8]

[7] *Winthrop Papers,* I. p. 3. Gorges' claim to power is mentioned by Sherley in a letter to Bradford in 1629, when referring to a patent obtained for Plymouth from Warwick and Gorges, "I am persuaded Sir Ferdinando (how loving and friendly soever he seems to be) knows he can, nay, proposes to overthrow at his pleasure all the patents he grants, but this being obtained, he will be frustrated of his intent." Bradford, *Letter Book,* p. 70.

[8] *Records of the Council for New England* [Deane], p. 59. This distinctly refers to the Council's grant, not the King's Patent.

On the same day, somewhat significantly, a patent, intended for Warwick but at his request transferred to his son Lord Rich, was submitted to a committee including Lord Gorges and Sir Ferdinando, to see that it did not prejudice other grants and to consider "how far the power of his Majesty's Patent for New England did extend for administering justice there in causes criminal or otherwise." [9]

At the next meeting Humfry was reproved for charging Sir Ferdinando falsely at the last meeting, because the letters to the Customs about ships and passengers had really been written by the Lord Treasurer acting upon their Charter, and the entry relating to this privilege in their minutes of 18 February, 1622, was shown to him. On this same occasion Sir Richard Saltonstall was desired "to make a map of the limits of those that live at Salem and the Massachusetts." [10] This points to a distinction between the grants for these two plantations. At the very next meeting Warwick was asked to find out what patents had been granted and to deliver up the seal, and it was then that the indignant Council decided not to meet again under his roof.

Although its presentation is not recorded, it is a reasonable inference that the map prepared by Saltonstall disclosed, on the best authority, that the entire territory granted to Warwick and his associates, without any reservation, had been obtained and included in the King's Letters Patent.

Gorges was faced with the *fait accompli* and knew that

9 *Records of the Council for New England* [Deane], p. 60.
10 *Ibid.*, p. 61.

his Majesty's Patent could not be revoked unless he was able to satisfy the Privy Council that it had been obtained by false representations.

The fact that the King's Letters Patent over-rode all other grants led Cradock to maintain that the Oldham-Dorrell grant was void in law and Winthrop to speak scoffingly of Gorges' claim to "a great part of the Bay of Massachusetts." [11] It also rendered it quite safe for the latter to deal with the Robert Gorges colonists as he pleased: Blackstone, who had shown compassion to the Winthrop emigrants in their misery immediately after they landed, found the "Lord-brethren" uncongenial companions—indeed, things seem to have been made so unpleasant for him that he moved away, selling the miserable pittance of fifty acres that the Court had seen fit to grant him,—whether in recognition of some legal claim or as a gift out of gratitude for his kindness does not appear.[12] Maverick, the son of their revered minister, though always in hot water and forever being lectured and fined, was a useful member of the community, so it was politic to deal leniently with him, but finally they were more than even he could endure, so he wrote that finding there were "those which take an inquisition-like course, by endeavouring to gather what they can from malcontented servants," he hoped "God will enable me in some measure to walk inoffensively, but finding by 10 years

---

[11] *History of New England*, I, p. 57.

[12] C. F. Adams, *Three Episodes*, p. 322, quotes Mather's scoff at Blackstone, that because he happened to sleep first in a hovel on a point of land there, he laid claim to all the ground where stands the metropolis of the whole English America, until the inhabitants gave him satisfaction. Yet as a settler on land granted by the Council he had a clear title, even if his residence was humble.

experience that I am eye sore to divers here, I have seriously resolved to remove hence." [13]   In the end he sought elsewhere freedom from religious and other persecution.

Walford, the blacksmith, was of a different social position; he was accused of insolence to the Court but by killing a wolf he was able to pay the fine inflicted; however, occasion was soon found to persecute him further and to drive him and his wife into banishment at the bitterest season of the year; in this way they rid themselves of all the Church of England men among the Gorges settlers; [14] of his company only Jeffries was allowed to remain because, having fallen out with Sir Ferdinando as we have seen, he bought favour by disclosing the letter Morton had written to him—in fact he turned "State's evidence," as it were.

If the view taken above of the transactions over the grant be correct there was ground for Gorges' charges: the Bay Company "obtained their first desires" under the Rosewell grant; but not satisfied, they "advanced themselves a step further by surreptitious means," enlarging their territory by the Warwick grant; and obtained his

13 *Winthrop Papers*, II, p. 308, dated March, 1640. One disgruntled settler declared only church members obtained justice, and "they were as good liue in Turkie as liue under such a government." *Ibid.*, p. 370.

14 C. F. Adams, *Three Episodes*, p. 321, hints that the ecclesiastical troubles that developed later at Wessaguscus were due to the "episcopalian" element existing among the Gorges settlers; finally the town "merged itself into the Puritan community which was pressing upon it on either side. As years went on it even passed from memory that the original settlement under Robert Gorges had proved a permanent one, and the closest historical scrutiny failed to detect, in record or tradition, a trace of Episcopal teachings. The leaven had wholly worked out."

Majesty's Letters Patent extending their domain from "sea to sea," three thousand miles, over-riding the heads of those who had had land allotted to them by King James.

Such was the case against the Massachusetts Bay Company, but they had taken away the original grants made by the Council for New England and these have now completely disappeared, as it was expedient for "them of the Bay" that they should; it is therefore impossible to say definitely how far the contents of these agreed with the statement in the Charter.

The equivocation and mal-practices charged against the Bay Company by Gorges were repeated by Robert Mason in his petition of 1676: "they did surreptitiously and unknown to the said Council, get the seal of the said Council affixed to a grant of certain lands; and did by their subtle practices, get a confirmation under the great seal of England." This shows that a suspicion existed that Warwick had used the seal improperly on this occasion, perhaps in the transfer of his own grant to the Company, as has been suggested above.

Nor was Mason the only one who held a poor opinion of the straightforwardness of the Company. Early in 1630 Edward Ashley was in treaty with the Council for New England for a grant of land on the Penobscot; this he eventually obtained in the names of John Beauchamp and Thomas Leverett on 13 March, 1629/30, shortly before the Planters sailed. Six days later Sherley wrote of it to Bradford: "the Salem partners here, as Mr. Humfries, Mr. Johnson, but chiefly Mr. Cradock and Mr.

Winthrop, would fain have joined with him [Ashley], and when that could not be, with us, in that business: but we not willing, and they failing, they said he would strip them of all trade in those parts; otherwise they so crossed him and us in the taking of the patent, as we could not have it, but to join their names with ours in it, though Knights, and men of good rank and near the King, spake in his behalf; and this I conceive they did only to bring it to pass, that they might join with us." [15]   The efforts of the "Salem partners" to obtain a share in the Penobscot grant proves that the Bay Company had no intention to abandon trading [16] and even then cast envious eyes on the land to the northward where, as Downing said, better timber was obtainable.[17]

Much has been said of the careless manner in which grants were drawn by the Council for New England; the uncertainty thereby caused to the position of the Bay Company was early recognized; on 12 December, 1630, Humfry, writing to Winthrop, mentions among the disadvantages of the site chosen the probable inability to sustain the claim to Massachusetts "in respect of the several titles and pretentions of several men." It was this

[15] Bradford, *Letter Book*, (Ed. 1906), p. 53. See reference to Beauchamp as agent for Plymouth above, p. 40.

[16] Osgood, *American Colonies*, I, p. 150, states that in 1630 "It was decided that henceforth that company should not directly engage in trade but should confine itself to regulating it."

[17] J. T. Adams, *Founding of New England*, pp. 182, 217, 242, deals with the unwarrantable extensions of the limits of the Massachusetts colony and in a note, p. 182, refers to Downing's suggestion. The Massachusetts men, with characteristic pride, claimed that the only cause of Gorges' complaints was envy; their settlement had prospered, his had failed. In their eyes no other reason was possible.

very fact that made Winthrop and his party deal sternly with any—whether agent or principal—who might be inclined to dispute the legality of their tenure.[18]

Concerning Robert Mason's charge in 1676 of "subtle practices" employed by the Company to obtain territory already granted to others, Haven writes: "In their answer the Massachusetts authorities deny the charge, no doubt with sincerity; but all the circumstances leave the impression upon the mind that, by his influence, perhaps by the management of the Earl of Warwick, advantages were gained which many, if not most, of the Council would have objected to," and he suggests that this and the trouble over the Connecticut Patent led to the unpleasantness between the Council and their President, Warwick.[19] We may leave it at that and deal with what happened after the Charter had been obtained.

[18] W. R. Scott, *Joint Stock Companies,* I, p. 312, asserts that the Charter was obtained simply because the Company feared that their title under the Council for New England might be assailed on account of overlapping grants—a theory unfamiliar to students. Humfry's statement shows that the possession of the Charter did not re-assure them.

[19] *Early History of Massachusetts,* Lowell Lectures, p. 154.

VII

CHARTER OF THE MASSACHUSETTS BAY COMPANY

IT may be fairly assumed that the prime movers in the effort to obtain a charter were Sir Richard Saltonstall and Isaac Johnson; they were large contributors to the Joint Stock—apparently Cradock, Aldersey and Whetcombe were the only others who ventured largely at the early period.

Some agreement must have been made with the original grantees under which their interests were taken over by the persons now undertaking the control of affairs, for three of the six grantees seem to have been but figureheads, lending their names as "gentlemen of blood" and taking no active part in business affairs, not even, as far as we know, attending any meetings; but now the "emigrant" element was in the ascendant among the active Adventurers who managed the business. There is no ground, however, for assuming that the Old Adventurers, who formed the "Generalitie" of the Company, were bought out by the new-comers—on the contrary, they retained their interest in the Old Stock and the Joint Stock, sat on committees and took active part in the transaction of business until the eve of the departure of the emigrants.[1]

[1] W. R. Scott, *Joint Stock Companies*, I, p. 201, asserts that "the shareholders resident in England" disposed of their holdings to the

The Charter supplies the names of those whom the original grantees "had associated with them," viz.: Sir Richard Saltonstall, Isaac Johnson, Samuel Aldersey, John Venn, Matthew Cradock, George Harwood, Increase Nowell, Richard Perry, Richard Bellingham, Nathaniel Wright, Samuel Vassall, Theophilus Eaton, Thomas Goffe, Thomas Adams, John Browne, Samuel Browne, Thomas Hutchins, William Vassall, William Pincheon, and George Foxcroft.[2] These, with "all such others as shall *hereafter* be admitted and made free of the Company and Society . . . shall be one body corporate and politic . . . by the name of the Governor and Company of the Massachusetts Bay in New England." [3]

By the strict letter of the Charter, on the day the Company came into existence it consisted of twenty-six [named] persons only. This indicates a clear division between the old and the new companies. However, it would appear that the Adventurers automatically became members of the new body, sitting in the Courts, acting on Committees, negotiating business and otherwise being entrusted with affairs but, as far as the records go, *without taking an oath as freemen.* Winthrop distinctly mentions *"the freemen in England"* and the deputies of the freemen in New England who took no oath that included emigrants. As late as 1638 the English shareholders retained their interests. [See below pp. 101–2.] Hubbard, *History of New England,* p. 108, says Winthrop and others bought the Patentees' rights and interest, but he must mean "in the plantation," not the shares.

2 All these names appear on the list of May, 1628, with the exception of Nathaniel Wright, the two Vassalls, the two Brownes, Thomas Goffe, Theophilus Eaton and William Pincheon. [See above, pp. 19, 20.]

3 *Massachusetts Records,* I, p. 10.

any judiciary powers.[4] Elsewhere he mentions that on his arrival in New England "we had no freemen besides the magistrates [i. e. the Assistants] that I remember, nor were there any considerable number of them for a good time after."[5] From these remarks we gather that freemen were sworn in England but none emigrated, yet the only reference to the subject in the Minutes is on 25 November, 1629, when at a General Court it was "thought fit to admit into the freedom of the Company Mr. Jo: Archer and Mr. Philip Nye," suggested as chaplains by Rev. John White.[6]

However, it must be assumed that the Company now incorporated included all the former Adventurers, numbering, as far as we know, fifty-seven. The officers specified in the Charter consisted of "the present Governor," Matthew Cradock, Thomas Goffe, Deputy Governor,[7] Sir Richard Saltonstall, Isaac Johnson, Samuel Aldersey, John Venn, John Humfry, John Endecott, Simon Whetcombe, Increase Nowell, Richard Perry, Nathaniel Wright, Samuel Vassall, Theophilus Eaton, Thomas Adams, Thomas Hutchins, John Browne, George Foxcroft, William Vassall, and William Pyncheon, Assistants.

---

[4] Winthrop, *Life of John Winthrop*, II, p. 431.

[5] *Ibid.*, p. 432. One hundred and sixteen became freemen at the earliest possible moment; they applied at the first General Court and were admitted at the second, the latter being held 18 May, 1631, before a year had elapsed after Winthrop's arrival. He admits that the express words of the Patent were not used when admitting freemen.

[6] *Massachusetts Records*, I, p. 62.

[7] Note that Cradock is styled "present governor" but Goffe is not called "present deputy governor"; the latter's name does not appear at any meeting until 5 March, 1628/9.

It will be seen that among the Assistants were included
Humfry, Endecott and Whetcombe, who were patentees,
but Bellingham and Samuel Browne, who were Associates,
were not included.

Matthew Cradock on 18 March, 1628/9, was sworn before a Master in Chancery to execute the office of Governor; the other officers were to be sworn before Cradock, so five days later the Deputy and eleven Assistants
then present were sworn as well as George Harwood, the
treasurer, while five other assistants were sworn at inter-
vals up to 17 June, the eighteenth was Endecott who was
in New England.[8]

New subscriptions must have been obtained as an entry
runs: "Warrant delivered the 30 March for moneys to
be paid to the Treasurer as followeth:

Mr. William Backhouse ..	25li	Mr. John Pococke	25li
Mr. Owen Rowe	25	Mr. George Foxcroft	25
Mr. John Bowles	25	Mr. Daniel Hodson	25
Mr. Robert Crane	25	Mrs. A. C.	25
Mr. Daniel Winche	25	Mr. William Crowther ...	25
Mr. Joseph Caron	25	Mr. John Venn	50
Mr. Richard Tuffnayle ..	50	Mr. Richard Young	50
Mr. John Davenport	25	Mr. Thomas Hutchins ...	25
Mr. Samuel Aldersey	75	Mr. Nathaniel Manesty ..	25
Mr. Richard Peerye	25	Mr. Theophilus Eaton ...	25
Mr. Nathaniel Wright ...	25	Mr. Christopher Coulson .	25
Mr. Richard Davis	25	Mr. Charles Whitchcote .	50
Mr. Increase Nowell	25	Mr. Edward Foorde	25
Mr. Edmond White	25	Mr. Samuell Vassall	50
Mr. John Humfrey	25	Mr. Simon Whitcombe ...	85
Mr. Hugh Peter	25	Mr. Edward Ironside	25
Mr. Joas Glover	25		

The total here subscribed is 1060li; probably Hubbard[9] had this list in mind as he mentions the unusual

[8] Wright and John Browne were sworn on 6 April, Pyncheon on
27, Aldersey on 30, Eaton on 21 May and Johnson on 17 June.
[9] Addenda to Haven's transcript of the Massachusetts Records
printed in *American Antiquarian Society Transactions*, III, p. 29.

sum of 85^{li} contributed by Whetcombe as well as Aldersey's 75^{li}; he also says the Governor gave 100^{li} and that
William Hubbard, his own father, and Mr. Wade [10] subscribed. The two latter, with the eight fresh names in
the above list, that of Thomas Hughson on a committee
appointed 23 March and three that first occur in the
Charter, Pyncheon, Samuel Browne and William Vassall,
bring the number of Adventurers known up to this date
to seventy, but there were probably others unrecorded.

It will be noticed that the amounts subscribed were for
the most part 25^{li}, but whether this sum entitled the subscribers to all the rights of Adventurers or was supple-
mental to a subscription already paid is uncertain; but
we do know that only those who had subscribed 50^{li} were
entitled to a grant of 200 acres of land.

[10] *History of New England,* p. 123. Probably this was Thomas,
father of Jonathan Wade, as the latter received land as an Adventurer afterwards.

VIII

INSTRUCTIONS TO ENDECOTT

BETWEEN the date of the sealing of the Charter and the election of officers on 13 May, 1629, there was an interval during which those who had been in charge of the business of the New England Company carried on the work which had already been begun and reference has been made to their undertakings.[1]

John Washborne was appointed secretary on 9 March and it may be inferred from the existing records that he found rough notes of contracts and similar arrangements from which he copied out what he considered essential, entering them somewhat promiscuously—e.g. an agreement with Vassall dated 16 March precedes a payment connected with the *Abigail* dated 23 February; probably he made notes of meetings just before he took office to enable him to compile "the minutes of the previous meeting" to be presented by him; records of agreements and of supplies follow until the end of the month when a formal meeting was held; the names of those present are then for the first time recorded. Frequent meetings took place during April; at that of the 6th a committee was appointed "for making orders and power for meet govern-

[1] See above, p. 25.

ment of New England, to write letters to Captain Endecott, to order divisions of lands and whatsoever may con-
cern the company's affairs," and another committee was
to divide those going out into "familyes." [2]

But the Company appears to have been in a dilemma;
the Charter required that the Governor and Council for
the Plantation should be elected at a formally summoned
meeting but the ships were expected to sail before that
could be held so it was necessary to inform Endecott of
the changes taking place and instruct him how to carry
on affairs, as the year for which he was appointed was
expiring. Apparently to solve this difficulty, they agreed
to write instructions on behalf of the Company which had
engaged him, i.e. the New England Company, and as Cradock was governor of this and of the incorporated Company, he could act as the mouthpiece of both. His letter,
dated 17 April, informed Endecott of the enlargement
of the Company; that he was appointed Governor; that
a Council for the Plantation had also been appointed, and
that certain concessions were to be made to the Old Planters. This, with a duplicate of the Charter and the new
Company's silver seal, went by the *George* on 4 May and
a copy with a postscript dated 21 April followed on the
Talbot on 11 May.

But meanwhile the General Court of 30 April had met
and confirmed the letter and postscript. At the same
meeting Endecott and Samuel Sharpe were formally proposed as candidates for the governorship and, by erection of hands, Endecott was elected; the Councillors were

[2] These entries are from the Addenda to Haven's paper mentioned
above. (See p. 62.)

voted for *en bloc* and the other matters mentioned in the letter which required to be authorized by the new Company were dealt with. It was further ordered that a copy of these acts and orders should be engrossed and despatched at once.

The annual election of officers took place on 13 May in accordance with the Charter and John Burges was elected secretary in place of Washbourne. On 18 May, at a meeting of the Court of Assistants, the acts of 30 April were amended as mentioned below and on 21 May a committee reported on the allotment of land to "adventurers in the Common Stock" and the Secretary was instructed to draw out at large the orders relating to the Governor and Council in New England as well as to the allotment of lands, and certain persons were appointed to attend to this and to affix the Company's seal. On 28 May full instructions were embodied in a letter but the name of the company on whose behalf it was written does not appear nor does it occur in the body of the letter, but the previous letter was confirmed and duplicates enclosed as well as the engrossed document and the forms of oaths that were to be administered. But the report of the Court's proceedings which were drawn out at large is carefully headed: "A General Court holden at London, the 30th Day of April, 1629, by the Governour & Company of the Mattachusetts Bay in New England." This is the first occasion on which the full title conferred by the Charter is used.

This document states that the patent this company had obtained gave them ample privileges and authorized them to deal with the affairs and government of the plantation; that thirteen persons there, reputed most wise, honest, expert and discreet, are to have the sole management of the government of the Company's affairs there and are to endeavour to settle the same as may make most for the glory of God, the furtherance of this hopeful plantation and the benefit of this so laudable work. They are to be entitled "the Governor and Council of London's Plantation in the Mattachusetts Bay in New England." Because of the merit, worth and good desert of Endecott and those lately gone over intending to reside, with the full consent and authority of the Court and by the erection of hands they have chosen and elected Endecott Governor of the Plantation. The other arrangements mentioned above are recorded and the Court authorized the appointment of a secretary and other subordinate officers there. Oaths were to be administered and the persons elected were to hold office for one year, with this amendment added on 21 May, "*or until such time as this Court shall think fit to make choice of any others to succeed in the place of them or any of them.*" This proviso shows that the Court intended to retain control and suggests that even then they had in mind a change of personnel. Authority was given to the officers in New England to fill for the unexpired term any vacancies caused by death or misdemeanour. Emphasis is laid on the fact that the Governor and Council were authorized by this act, *grounded on the power derived from his Majesty's Charter* to ordain reasonable laws, not repugnant or contrary to those of England, for the punishment of offenders and the orderly government of the inhabitants there.[3]

By the above communication the Massachusetts Bay Company officially endorsed the instructions given by the New England Company to tide over the interim.

[3] *Massachusetts Records,* I, p. 361, *et seq.*

IX

MEMBERSHIP OF THE MASSACHUSETTS BAY COMPANY

AT the annual election mentioned above "by the consent of the Generality" Cradock was elected Governor, Goffe Deputy Governor, Harwood Treasurer and sixteen of the Assistants were also elected, but as two of them were out of the land, Endecott and John Browne, in their places were elected John Pocock [1] and Christopher Coulson.

The Generality were summoned "by tickets" to attend on 17 June to consider a matter of great importance. The "bringing in of moneys" was the subject first dealt with on that occasion, for their treasury had been depleted by the expenses incurred for the patent and in fitting out the ships, etc. Several alternative courses were suggested: to increase their former subscriptions; to invite others to underwrite; to borrow money for a time "to supply the occasions"; to take up money at interest; and, as a separate suggestion which was accepted, that those here present do furnish 200^{li} or 100^{li} apiece, to have allowance for it.

1 See above, p. 66.

Those in Court [2] who "underwrit to lend" were:

Sir R. Saltonstall	100li	Simon Whetcombe	25li
Mr. Governor	150	Thomas Hutchins	25
Mr. Deputy	50	Edward Cooke	50
Richard Perry	25	Daniel Ballard	25
Thomas Adams	50	Edmund White	20
Increase Nowell	25	Joseph Caron	25
George Harwood	50	Samuel Aldersey	50
Richard White	25	Thomas Andrewes	25
Mr. Clark	25		

This amounts to 745li and the list gives us four new names: Andrewes, Richard White, Cooke and Clark, bringing up the number of Adventurers to seventy-four.

As 1500li was required to discharge debts other Adventurers were asked to subscribe.

In order to clear up the confused state of accounts eight Adventurers were selected to compose a committee of auditors, four constituting a quorum.[3] Another committee was to reduce "all former orders into a method," probably this means codifying the standing orders of the several bodies that had been in control, for on this were persons who had been active members of the earlier companies. The secretary of the Company was to enter all "in a fair book to be kept for the purpose, according to the usage of other Companies." In such manner the Company's affairs were placed on a business-like footing.

A ship of 400 tons was in the market but as the Com-

---

[2] *Massachusetts Records*, I, p. 46.

[3] Osgood, *American Colonies*, I, p. 133, quotes this appointment of auditors as evidence of the establishment of a business undertaking, but these were not professional auditors such as would be employed now, but eight Adventurers empowered to act on this occasion only; at the end of a month, having dealt with this matter, they ceased to exist as a committee and no others appear to have been appointed, and the Governor and Deputy Governor acted instead of auditors on 29 October following.

pany was out of funds Adventurers subscribed for either eighths or sixteenths, one-eighth being entered for the Company as a whole; this was afterwards offered, when that body was short of cash, to the intending emigrants, but we have no record that they took it over. This ship was the *Eagle,* afterwards renamed the *Arbella.*

Endecott had complained that traders were supplying the natives with weapons and as this traffic had been forbidden by proclamation in 1622 the Company proposed to request the King to renew this order; accordingly a petition was presented to the Privy Council, pointing out that their Patent granted them the privilege of carrying over men and provisions for a plantation in New England for seven years and that ships freighted this year carried more passengers than was expected, "many poor people pressing aboard with cattle but no provisions; the Company having depended too much upon the industry of their servants, had sent less victuals than were requisite and through slothfulness and neglect in planting corn, many had died, and the rest, about a thousand persons, were afraid of being surprised by savages who had been supplied with guns by interlopers, so they prayed for a licence for one year to carry over provisions until the crops were available next season and for the renewal of the proclamation against this disorderly trade in weapons." It is worthy of comment that this petition is very misleading; poor people if they had cattle could not ship them without special licence; there could not have been anything approaching a thousand settlers at this date even including the Plymouth men and scattered settlers, and if they had licence under the Charter for seven years and the first year had not expired how was it necessary to ask for another for the present year? However, they had sufficient influence, probably through the Lord Keeper who was brother-in-law to one of the actual petitioners, to obtain a favourable reply to both requests except that only certain specified provisions were allowed under this licence.[4]

But the most important business brought forward was the reading of propositions conceived, it is said, by the Governor, in order to advance the plantation, to encourage persons of worth and quality to emigrate with their families and for other weighty reasons, that the government of the plantation should be transferred to those that shall inhabit there and not continue in subordination to the Company in England *as it now is.*

The words of this proposition, made on 28 July, the very first hint contained in the records of a startling proposal, require careful scanning. They can be construed only to mean that the emigrants were to have power to deal with local affairs, such as happened on the plantation—concerning which matters they would not be required to consult the Company in England; they cannot be construed to mean that by delegating that much power the Company in England ceased to exist. Distance and difficulties of communication required a certain amount of freedom in the matter of local government and if "men of worth and quality" were in charge they could be entrusted with such affairs. Bearing in mind that it is

---

[4] *State Papers, Colonial,* V, 106. Can it be that the "patent" granting the privilege for seven years was the indenture issued to Sir Walter Yonge in 1622/3 which would have expired about this period?

claimed that the Patentees had the Charter altered so as to free them from having their head-quarters in England, it is notable that on this occasion, nearly five months after the Charter came into force, it is expressly stated that the government of the plantation is now in subordination to the Company in London.

But this guarded proposition, giving a measure of local government, did not meet with unanimous approval. It occasioned some debate and met with so much disapprobation that, owing to the many and considerable consequences depending upon it, further consideration was postponed to an adjourned meeting, meanwhile those present were instructed to write out their reasons for and against the propositions and present them at the next General Court, when "reduced to heads and maturely considered of" the Company would make its final decision, but all were "desired to carry the business secretly that the same be not divulged." The reason for this secrecy was doubtless the fear that the authorities might learn of the scheme and prevent its execution.[5]

Obviously the opposition was considerable and could not be overborne, so to meet this situation those who desired to have the Government and the Charter transferred

---

[5] *Massachusetts Records,* I, p. 46. It is worth noting that the monthly courts in August and September were merely adjournments of the General Court and were not the usual Courts of Assistants. The July Court was unusually well attended, eleven Assistants and nine of the "generalitie" are named. On 28 August fifteen Assistants were present, and one more attended next day. The Generality present on those days numbered six and three respectively. Cradock did not attend these meetings. When the transfer was finally considered on 15 October twelve Assistants attended and eleven of the Generality are named, including five whose names do not occur previously, among them Dudley and Winthrop.

to the Plantation took steps to strengthen their hands before the next meeting; to this end was drawn up the "Cambridge Agreement" which, after expressing their reasons for emigrating in person, bound them to remove with their families to New England on condition that "before the last of September next the whole Government, together with the patent for the said Plantation, be first by order of the Court, legally transferred and established to remain with us and others which shall inhabit upon the said Plantation." This was signed by twelve men. Of these Saltonstall, Nowell, William Vassall, Pyncheon, Johnson, Humfry and Colbron occur as Adventurers before this date; Sharpe, Dudley and Winthrop, were present at later Courts but West and Kellam Browne do not appear as Adventurers at all. Two days after this document was signed the adjourned meeting of the General Court took place, when those present were informed that the special cause of their meeting was to "give answer to divers gentlemen intending to go into New England, whether or no the chief government of the Plantation, together with the Patent, should be settled in New England or here." Again the inference is that some part of the government was to remain in England while the Cambridge Agreement mentions the "whole government." It was ordered "that this afternoon Mr. Wright, Mr. Eaton, Mr. Adams and Mr. Spurstowe and such others as they should think fit to call unto them, whether they were of the Company or not, [were] to consider of arguments against the settling of the chief government in New England. And on the other side, Sir Richard Saltonstall, Mr. Johnson, Captain Venn and such others as they shall call unto them, to prepare arguments for the settling of the said government in New England;" to meet the next morning at 7 o'clock to consider the arguments and at 9 o'clock to report to the whole Company. At the General Court next day many were present and the committees openly debated their arguments and reasons. After a long debate the question was put: those desiring the patent and government of the plantation transferred to New England, "so as it may be done legally, hold up your hands; so many as will not, hold up your hands. Whereas by erection of hands, it appeared by the general consent of the Company, that the government and patent should be settled in New England an order was drawn up accordingly." [6]

From the above account we glean the names of the leaders of the opposition to the transfer and find that it had considerable strength; to the last it was held, to judge from the record, that it could not be done legally and at the next adjournment, although the business of the transfer was deferred until Saltonstall, Johnson and others came up to London, a committee was appointed to deal with the matter and their first instruction was "to take advice of learned counsel whether the same can be legally done or no," but there is no record that any opinion was given. This is an important point as modern lawyers hold that the Charter did not sanction the transfer.

Disputes have arisen over this question of the legality of the transfer. It has been claimed that before application was made for a patent an elaborate scheme was

6 *Massachusetts Records*, I, p. 51.

devised whereby the colony about to be established would be entirely free from any control by a body remaining in England. In support of this the chief evidence quoted is a paragraph in Winthrop's pamphlet on "Arbitrary Government." In this he makes this remarkable statement about the last clause of the Charter relating to the government of the Plantation. "For it being the manner for such as procured patents for Virginia, Bermudas and the West Indies, to keep the chief government in the hands of the company residing in England (*and so this was intended and with much difficulty we got it abscinded*) this clause is inserted in this and all other patents whereby the Company in England might establish a Government and Officers here in any form used in England, as Governor and Council, Justice of Peace, Mayor, Bailiffs, etc., and accordingly Mr. Endecott and others with him were established a Governor and Council here, before the Government was transferred hither." [7]

This treatise was written to confute claims that were in no way dependent upon the wording of this part of the Charter; the clause in brackets was obviously inserted as an afterthought; it was casually made and is contradicted by the context; he says the clause was inserted in the Charter and was acted upon. Yet it is claimed that the clause was abscinded before the Patent reached its final form because the applicants desired to cut themselves free from the control of those in London and that because they got it expunged they were authorized by the Charter to so act legally.

It is a flimsy basis for such a claim; it was but hear-

[7] Winthrop, *Life of John Winthrop*, II, p. 443.

say, for Winthrop was not present, it was repeated many years after the event for a different purpose and it does not accord with the evidence of the early records. It has been pointed out that if the applicants for the Charter had its wording altered for the purpose alleged they successfully hoodwinked both the English government and many of their own associates.[8] Downing, bred to the law, and as likely as Winthrop to know the course of events, if the alteration had been made would have put forward the simple plea of the absence of this clause when he advised those summoned under the *Quo Warranto* in 1635 and would not have used the words quoted below when writing in 1633 regarding a new charter and the desire of the colonists to retain the protection of their natural Prince.[9] Moreover, for six months the Company acted as if no such meaning could be read into the Charter and they even doubted whether the proposed transfer could be legally accomplished under it. In the document drawn up to inform Endecott they stated officially that the Charter authorized them to appoint officers for ordering and governing their affairs "both in England and in the places [specified] and granted unto us by his Majesty's said charter;" and the Company in London proceeded, as Winthrop says, to appoint Endecott and others. When Cradock first mooted the change the suggestion was that the government of the plantation should not continue "in subordination to the Company here, *as now it is*," and later it was considered how the transfer "may be done to

---

[8] J. T. Adams, *Founding of New England*, p. 139. He states the case quite clearly.
[9] See below, p. 96.

correspond with and not prejudice the government here."
As has been said above, the transference of the government was not accepted by all as sanctioned by the Charter but was a question of so much uncertainty that it required a formal and public debate of the *pros* and *cons*
of its wisdom while even its legality was disputed, none of
which would have been pertinent if the wording of the
Charter admitted of the reading put upon it later. There
are other small items pointing to the fact that this bold
scheme could not have been in the minds of the promoters
before the Charter was obtained and supporting rather
the theory that it was an afterthought—that when the
emigrants desired complete freedom they sought, and believed they had found, a loop-hole and desired counsel's
opinion on the legality of their interpretation. As far as
we know, that opinion was not submitted to the body that
ordered it taken, so it is quite possible that it was ad-
verse; the leaders may even have decided to risk the transfer and chance its discovery by the authorities when too
late—as we are aware the latter, when they did find it
out, took legal steps in the matter. Legal opinions have
been given by modern lawyers to the effect that the decision of the Judges in 1677 was not in accordance with
the law—the Judges' decision was that as the title in the
Charter, "the Governor and Company . . . in New
England," created them a Corporation upon the place,
ignoring the application of the words "in New England"
to the situation of "Massachusetts Bay"; yet before the
transfer this title was used in the instructions of 30 April,
1629.[10]

It may, however, be admitted that the Charter under-

[10] See above, p. 19.

went some alteration in wording during its progress through its several stages. Mr. Charles Deane calls attention to a curious discrepancy between the docket of the Sign Manual and the Charter itself; a docket was intended to place before the King a brief statement of the contents of the document he was to sign. In this case it stated that the Charter contained clauses for electing "of Governors and officers *here in England* and powers to make laws for settling the Government and Magistracy for the plantation there." [11] This clearly contemplated the existence of headquarters with officials in England with the government of the plantation subordinate to them. But in the Charter the words "here in England" are omitted and a long sentence inserted "for the settling of the forms and ceremonies of government and magistracy fit and necessary for the said plantation and the inhabitants there." This does away with the "here" and "there" of the docket but leaves the last word "there" as applying to the situation of the inhabitants. It seems possible that this was intentional for the purpose of misleading the official whose duty it was to compare the two documents.

Whatever may have been the actual date of the inception of the idea, the majority of those present on 29 August voted for the transfer, *provided* it could be legally done and, with or without counsel's opinion, this vote was accepted as settling the matter, for on 15 October reference is casually made to the fact that "by a former order the government is to be transferred to New England."[12]

But the legality or illegality of their proceedings

11 *Massachusetts Historical Society Proceedings*, 1869/70, p. 173.
12 *Massachusetts Records*, I, p. 55.

troubled their consciences little, the attainment of so pious a purpose condoned many things. With the Charter, which secured to them their territory and their powers of government, they played fast and loose; if it furthered their aim it was sacrosanct, if it did not it was hidden from prying eyes [13] and treated as a dead letter. According to it the Governor must be elected annually at a special meeting which must be held on the last Wednesday of Easter term, yet they called a meeting on 19 October, 1629, for the express purpose of electing a governor. In the absence of Cradock, then holding office, whose presence was requisite, John Winthrop was elected and other offices were filled; incidentally, the holders of these offices were changed at will at subsequent meetings in England regardless of the Charter's requirements. Not only was this breach committed but no legally convened meeting could be held in the spring of 1630 because they were all at sea, so Winthrop continued in office for eighteen months, contrary to the provisions of the Charter.

It may be contended that he was simply elected Governor of the plantation as Endecott had been before him, but he sat in the Governor's chair at subsequent meetings in England which were partly devoted to English business, and Governor Cradock even submitted to him an account of moneys expended on behalf of the Company.

Other evidence will be found elsewhere of the treatment the Charter received and how several breaches of its strict commands were made and its provisions ignored.

13 See below, p. 117.

X

JOINT STOCK AND THE UNDERTAKERS

THE special and only occasion for which the meeting of 15 October, 1629, was called was the consideration of "the settling the trade in New England . . . for the encouragement as well of the Adventurers in the Joint Stock here, as of those who already are, and others who intend to go over in person to be planters there, and for their mutual correspondence and behoof and the advancement of the Plantation to the end which was first intended." [1]

The Joint Stock here mentioned requires consideration because of its importance and the fact that all who have written upon the Company have failed to grasp the distinction between the several funds or "stocks"—the Common Stock, the General Stock, the Joint Stock, the Old Stock, the New Stock, or whatever they chanced to be called. It must be admitted that it is difficult to differentiate them. "Joint Stock" is not used in the modern sense but represents a fund distinct from the Common or the General Stock subscribed by the Adventurers. As early as May, 1628, persons were held responsible for their "several and general stock" when money was subscribed to the "joint stock." [2] On 2 March, 1628/9, it is

---

[1] *Ibid.*, p. 55.
[2] Felt, *Annals of Salem*, I, p. 508.

recorded that the Boston men wished to underwrite 25^{li} a man to the "Joint Stock" and send out the equivalent of 250^{li}, which though prejudicial to the "General Stock" was to the advantage of the Plantation. A distinction is clearly made here between the Joint Stock and the General Stock and, occurring at such an early date, it suggests that the original Joint Stock had been formed by a combination of the rights and possessions of the Dorchester Company with contributions of some sort made by members of the New England Company—a hint of this is found in Cradock's reference to the Dorchester men giving what they had on the Plantation "to go upon the account of their stock intended," [3] and also by the fact that Rev. John White was appointed on the committee to value this stock.[4]

When the subject of the Joint Stock was brought up before a full General Court in October "due and mature consideration" was given to it, and "after a long debate, and sundry opinions given, and reasons why the Joint Stock (which had borne the brunt of the charge hitherto, and was likely to bear more) should have certain commodities appropriated thereunto, for reimbursement and defrayment thereof, and divers objections being made to those reasons, all which was largely discussed and well weighed, the Court, in conclusion, for accommodation of both parties, fell upon a moderation, as followeth, viz:

"That the Company's Joint Stock shall have the trade of beaver and all other furs in those parts solely, for the term of seven years from this day, for and in consider-

---

[3] *Winthrop Papers*, I, p. 126.
[4] See below, p. 85.

ation of the charge that the Joint Stock hath undergone already and is yet annually to bear, for the advancement of the plantation.

"That for the charge of fortifications the Company's Joint Stock to bear one half and the planters [to defray] the other, viz. for ordnance, munition, powder, etc: but for labourers in building of forts, etc. all men to be employed in an equal proportion, according to the number of men upon the plantation, and so to continue until such fit and necessary work be finished.

"That the charge of the ministers now there, or that shall hereafter go to reside there, as also the charge of building convenient churches, and all other public works upon the plantation, be in like manner indifferently borne, the one half by the Company's Joint Stock for the said term of 7 years, and the other half by the planters.

"That the ordnance already provided for fortifications be rated as they cost, as also all powder and munition whatsoever concerning arms, so as the same be delivered there for public use; and this to be accounted as part of the Joint Stock of the Company.

"All which being several times read, was by Mr. Governor put to the question, and by general consent, by erection of hands, was agreed and concluded on and ordered accordingly." [5]

At the Court of Assistants held next day the business before the meeting was to decide, owing to the transfer of the government of the plantation to New England "what government shall be held at London, whereby the future charge of the Joint Stock may be cherished and preserved

[5] *Massachusetts Records,* I, p. 55.

and the body politic of the Company remain and increase.

"What persons shall have the charge of the managing of the Joint Stock, both at London and in New England; wherein it is conceived fit that Captain Endecott continue the government there, unless just cause to the contrary.[6]

"These and other things were largely discussed; and it was thought fit and natural that the government of persons be held there, the government of trade and merchandize to be here;

"That the Joint Stock being mutual, both here and there, that some fit persons be appointed for managing thereof in both places." [7]

This quotation is given at length as it so clearly sets forth the points connected with the Joint Stock which were to be considered; it also shows that it was held in common,—mutually,—by those remaining in England and those emigrating, proving incidentally that there was no intention to terminate the existence of the Company in England whose duties are here defined. That body politic was to remain and increase and it was to have the sole management of trade—as a body they proposed to continue trading as will be seen later on.

The above propositions were considered but as there was "a great debt owing by the Joint Stock" it was decided to clear this before the government was transferred; auditing of the accounts was suggested but time being short the Governor and Deputy were asked to prepare an estimate of the debts to submit to the next meeting.

[6] This reference to Endecott is obscure but it may be that a party existed that wished to retain him in power in New England.
[7] *Massachusetts Records*, I, p. 56.

At that meeting the whole subject was referred to
a committee, because it would take up too much of the
Court's time. They were to meet and make propositions
in writing for the good of the plantation; if they dis-
agreed on any matter it was to be submitted to the umpir-
age of certain ministers who would make a report in writing as in conscience they thought best for the good of
the work and the encouragement of both planters and
Adventurers; articles between these parties to implement
the decision were drawn up by Mr. White, the Counsellor,
and approved by the General Court the next day. There-
upon two committees [8] and umpires were appointed. For
the planters Saltonstall, Winthrop, Dudley, Johnson and
Humfry; for the Adventurers Cradock, Aldersey, Wright,
Hutchins and Venn; umpires, Mr. White the Counsellor,
Mr. White of Dorchester and Mr. Davenport. Time was
short; fresh matters might be suggested for consideration; the Committee was to report on those matters upon
which they agreed and other things might be submitted
to them in writing.

On 25 November the Committee reported through the
Governor that "notwithstanding there had been all good
concordancy and fair proceeding" yet by reason of the
"greatness of the business and the smallness of the supplies they could not bring the same to a wished effect";
however, they presented propositions for consideration.
They estimated the arrears at 3000^{li} and upwards; they
required 2000^{li} for the Company's servants, 500^{li} each
for merchandise for trade and munitions. 1900^{li} was still

8 "Committees" is used in the Records for individual members of a
committee.

due from subscribers and about 900^{li} due from freight on ships. Money was therefore required "either to revive the old stock or to raise a new." They suggested three methods: (a) *former Adventurers* should double their *former* subscription; (b) the servants, cattle, provisions, etc., of the Joint Stock to be sold and the underwriters to be paid according to shares; (c) or, lastly, the Old Stock to be placed in the hands of undertakers on agreed conditions, they to manage affairs, standing profit and loss, and at the end of seven years to pay the underwriters their principal; others might subscribe to this but the undertakers should be few. To encourage the underwriters the Committee suggested they should have: (1) half of the beaver-trade; (2) the sole making of salt; (3) the sole transportation of passengers, goods, etc., at reasonable rates; (4) a reasonable profit on supplies for a magazine for the inhabitants on the plantation.

The consideration of these proposals was postponed to a larger meeting summoned "by tickets." On 30 November the officers, including all Assistants, and twenty-five of the "Generality" attended, the debt was given as 2500^{li} and for present maintenance of the plantation 1500^{li} was required. The Adventurers refused to double their subscriptions but it was agreed to choose ten persons, five of the Adventurers and five of the planters, as undertakers and to grant the four privileges mentioned above as "appropriated to the Joint Stock." A committee was appointed to value the Joint Stock.

They reported the next day. The disbursement of public charges, as transporting ministers and their families, ammunition, etc., were not now to be valued [9] to the undertakers; divers servants sent proved unprofitable, and cattle and provisions had miscarried through lack of experience so that, debts being cleared, the value was about one third part of the whole sum that had been adventured from the first to the present day. "Upon examination and long debate" this was allowed by all the Court.

The Court agreed that the Old Adventurers, in lieu of this abatement of two-thirds of their adventures, should have a double portion of land, according to the first proportion of 200 acres for 50^{li}, and have liberty to subscribe, before January next, or for country Adventurers before February, what they pleased; "any of the said Adventurers may take out their adventures at the aforesaid rate." Others, with the consent of any three of the undertakers could subscribe what they pleased "to be traded in the Joint Stock (upon such allowance to the common stock for public uses, in regard that they shall bear no part in the former losses,) as the said Adventurers, or three of them, shall agree with them for, from time to time," payment to be made as agreed by the undertakers or any three of them.

As the undertakers would bear the greatest charge and burden and all other Adventurers would have equal part of the gain if any, the undertakers were to have five per cent of the clear gains of the Joint Stock after the deduction of costs.

[9] Perhaps the phrase used here led the Massachusetts Court in 1650 into believing that the Joint Stock was sold to the undertakers, but the context shows that these charges were merely not to be included in the valuation made to adjust the claims of the Old Adventurers.

The Joint Stock being so managed, it with the profits was to be divided proportionately to every one at the end of seven years; all privileges were then to cease and all persons would then be at liberty to dispose of their parts in the Joint Stock.

This matter has been dealt with at length as there has been so much misunderstanding of the situation. It is obvious that the "Old Adventurers" must have been those who subscribed to the Company at the first, under the Rosewell grant, and were the senders of the ministers, etc., they did not "dispose of their shares" to the New Adventurers, or Planters; the wording of the agreement shows that they were not at liberty to do so before the seven years expired, though they had the right to take out one-third of their adventure in cash; but they retained their interest and undertook to join in carrying on the trading business of the Company by means of the Joint Stock. Meanwhile, for their trouble in the business the *Undertakers* appointed were to have as remuneration five per cent of the clear profits, and at the end of seven years the principal with the rest of the profits was to be divided among the Adventurers in both countries according to the amount they had subscribed.[10]

[10] W. R. Scott, *Joint Stock Companies,* misunderstands the whole subject of this Joint Stock, assuming these agreements applied to the property of the entire Company as a Joint Stock company in the modern sense; he makes many minor errors, e.g.: "the residents in England had [before 1631] disposed of their holdings to those who had emigrated" [I, p. 201]. The sum paid down was "one-third of that adventured" [II, p. 311]. Complaining shareholders were told they would receive, besides one-third of their capital, a double portion of land [p. 414], "the Undertakers were not bound . . . to make good previous losses" [*Ibid.*]. "Instead of the monopolies [the Undertakers] were to receive 5% of the profits." At the end of seven years the assets of the Joint Stock and any

It took "much entreaty of the Court" to persuade ten gentlemen to accept the onerous positions of Undertakers but those finally appointed were, from among the Planters: Winthrop, Saltonstall, Johnson, Dudley and Revell; from the Adventurers: Cradock, Wright, Eaton, Goffe and Young; Aldersey was appointed treasurer, "all moneys which shall come in to the Joint Stock, or that shall be given to the Common Stock, [i.e. the newly established fund,] shall be paid unto him, and to be issued out under the hands of the said Undertakers or any three of them." Instructions were given to the Undertakers concerning shipping to be supplied and the rates to be charged for passengers and goods; for the management of the magazine, allowing a charge of 25^{li} in the hundred above all charges, and Planters were "to have liberty to dispose of *their part of the beavers* at their own will." As the Court "could not set down directions for everything" other matters were left to the discretion of the majority of the Undertakers; this, of course, included the monopoly of salt which required no special orders at the moment.[11]

It is, therefore, quite clear that the Joint Stock did receive the privileges as at first proposed. Regarding the beaver-trade, Pyncheon mentions an order of the Court "that there should be but one in a town to trade in beaver," [12] which suggests that the Government kept con-

profits remaining after payments due to the Adventurers had been made, were to be divided amongst the Colonists . . . property not divisible to be transferred to the Governor and Assistants on behalf of the whole body of settlers. [*Ibid.*] Not one of these statements is correct.

11 *Massachusetts Records,* I, p. 66.

12 *Pyncheon Papers,* Massachusetts Historical Collections, 2nd Series, IV, p. 157.

trol of that business, possibly dividing the skins between the Planters and Adventurers; there is no reference to salt-making in the Records until 1641 and there is none to the transport of goods or to a magazine but about the expiration of the seven years certain gentlemen in England were planning to establish a magazine for the benefit of the inhabitants on the Plantation.[13]

From the above it is evident that the fund described as the "Joint Stock" had defrayed the expenses of the ministers, servants and supplies as all of these were sent out before May, 1629, the season then being ended; that they had begun to erect forts and provide munitions, all of which had been undertaken while the New England Company officers remained in charge, so the members of that Company must be identical with the "Old Adventurers."

An important item in the above agreement is in the next to last paragraph: "what orders and directions [the greater number of the Undertakers] shall set down, shall be accounted legal, and to be duly observed until it shall be thought fit by the Court to alter or determine the same." This shows that the Court then existing in England [14] was to continue to function and was to have control over the actions of all the Undertakers, and it evidently provides that until information of the orders promulgated in New England could reach them, obedience to such orders would not be counted illegal should they be subsequently disallowed.

[13] *Massachusetts Historical Society Collections,* 5th Series, I, p. 231.
[14] No court to alter and determine the orders and directions of the emigrant Undertakers is known to have existed in the Colony, and it is shown below that during the seven years in which they held office the Massachusetts Records contain no reference whatever to them.

Finally it is stated that "if those that intend to inhabit upon the plantation shall, before the first of January next, take upon them all the said engagements and other charges of the Joint Stock, then the power and privileges of the undertakers to determine and all trade, etc., to be free." That the emigrants did not take over the engagements of the Joint Stock is evident from the statement of Dudley in his letter of 12 March, 1630/1; after reference to the return to England of Revell and the death of Johnson he says: "so that there now were left of the five undertakers but the Governor, Sir Richard Saltonstall and myself;" he describes their misfortunes, adding: "all which . . . weakened our estates, especially the estates of the undertakers who were three or four thousand [? li] engaged in the joint stock, which was not now above so many hundreds." [15]

The settlement of the Joint Stock and the management of the whole business was of so great consequence that it was brought up for confirmation at a General Court held on 15 December, attended by the Deputy, Humfry, nine Assistants and seventeen of the Generality. "Upon debate whereof some exceptions were taken by those who had doubled their adventures, conceiving themselves to be wronged in having both their sums drawn down to so low a rate as a third part; alleging that the second sum was paid upon a proposition of trade which went not forward, and not as unto the joint stock of the plantation."

"This business received a large discussion, and Captain Waller and Mr. Vassall were content to give the first 50^{li} to the plantation, so as their other 50^{li} might go on wholly

[15] *Force Reprint,* p. 11. The letters "ties" after the figures are unintelligible.

in this new stock; but forasmuch as this concerned divers others who were in the same case, and that it could not be done without alteration of the act made the 30th November, which was done by a General Court, upon mature and deliberate consideration, and that the undertakers would not continue their undertaking but upon the same conditions which were then propounded and concluded on . . . [the question was put and by vote] every particular of the former Court was ratified and confirmed. And the matter in difference with them who had doubled their adventures being no more to each of them than between 50^{li} and 33^{li} 6^s 8^d, was by mutual consent referred to the three ministers here present, Mr. Davenport, Mr. Nye, and Mr. Archer, who are to reconcile the same between the new Adventurers and them." [16]

Here the Joint Stock and the New Stock are put in juxtaposition and the meaning of the former term made clear—the fund was to be used for the benefit of the plantation and, seemingly, was contributed jointly by the Old Adventurers—former members of the New England Company—and the New Adventurers, otherwise the emigrants.

Commenting upon this Johnson wrote on 17 December: "We had a court on Tuesday at which was three or four hours debated whether those that added to their subscriptions before should have it now fully ended, and after three or four hours strong debate it was concluded against them so as now we shall I hope go securely on with the merchants." [17]

The next meeting of the General Court was held on 10

[16] *Massachusetts Records,* I, p. 67.
[17] *Winthrop Papers,* I, p. 31.

February when we again find the distinction between the
funds of the Company. "Forasmuch as the fur+herance
of the plantation will necessarily require a great and con-
tinual charge, which cannot with convenience be defrayed
out of the Joint Stock of the Company, which is ordained
for the maintenance of the trade, without endangering
the same to be wasted and exhausted, it was therefore pre-
pounded that a Common Stock should be raised from such
as bear good affection to the plantation, and the propagation thereof, and the same to be employed only in
defrayment of public charges, as maintenance of ministers, transportation of poor families, building of churches
and fortifications, and all other public and necessary occasions of the plantation." [18]   Here the Joint Stock is
stated to be for trade and the new "Common Stock" was
for philanthropic purposes. It was decided that two hundred acres should be allotted for every fifty pounds subscribed, for smaller sums in the same proportion. Harwood was chosen treasurer of this Common Stock and
authorized to issue out moneys "upon warrant under the
hands of any two or more of the undertakers." A cir-
cular was to be issued under the Company's seal, asking
for subscriptions for "so laudable and charitable work."
"The allotments were not to prejudice the rights of other
adventurers but if for good or weighty reasons and for
the benefit of the plantation in general, there shall be
occasion to alter any man's allotment, the said party is
to have such due recompense for the same as, in the wisdom of the Governor and Company there resident, shall
be thought reasonable and expedient."

18 *Massachusetts Records,* I, p. 68.

This paragraph emphasizes the strictly local control by the "Governor and Company 'here resident" who were not in this case required to refer the matter to the Company in England, but the exception suggests that the rule was to submit such matters to them.

XI

THE GOVERNMENT IN LONDON

THAT a Company in England distinct from that of the Plantation was contemplated is clear from the Records and that it continued in existence during the allotted seven years there can be little doubt.

The Court of Assistants of 16 October, 1629, "was appointed to treat and resolve, that upon the transferring of the government to New England, what government shall be held at London, whereby the future charge of the Joint Stock may be cherished and preserved, and the body politic of the Company remain and increase.

"What persons shall have the managing of the Joint Stock, both at London and in New England, . . . it was thought fit and natural that the government of persons be held there, the government of trade and merchandize here. That the Joint Stock being mutual, both here and there, that some fit persons be appointed for the management thereof in both places."

As we have seen five English Adventurers were among the undertakers appointed and to them was entrusted the management of the trade and merchandise. Downing brings out the distinction between the two sections of the Company and proves the existence of a body in London holding power several years later. Writing in 1633 to

Secretary Coke he says that the aims of the Virginia settlers were purely for profit while the Massachusetts planters went "some to satisfy their own curiosity in point of conscience, others, which was more general, to transport the Gospel to those heathen that never heard thereof. . . . The whole trade of the plantation is maintained by such undertakers as remain in England. Those that govern the plantation have both lands and children here [in England]. Divers others are in reversion and are in hope of lands here for themselves or their children. The undertakers here will persuade the planters to accept a new patent and thereby be bound to transport no masts, etc. for [nor ?] cordage and shipping but into old England. One thing will be humbly desired of his Majesty in this patent, aid against all foreign enemies, and that the patent be enlarged a little to the north where is the best firs and timber. It is a causeless fear without precedent that a colony planted in a strange land was ever so foolishly besotted as to reject the protection of their natural Prince . . . Let this Corporation but enjoy the liberty of their patent and to choose their own officers as every corporation doth here, then shall this kingdom gain by the fruits of their labours that commodious trade of cordage, pitch and tar." [1]

It may be that Downing over-rated the powers of persuasion of the English Adventurers but that they existed as a body and took an active interest in affairs is here shown by Winthrop's brother-in-law, then residing in England, who acted at times as legal adviser to the Adven-

[1] *Historical MSS. Commission*, Report XII, Appendix II, p. 36, quoted in *Calendar of State Papers*, Colonial, Addenda [1574–1674], p. 159.

turers. It was indeed essential that an English Company should remain in being, composed chiefly of holders of the Joint Stock, in order to deal with the beaver trade, the magazine, the salt monopoly and the other duties allotted to them. Nor can their non-existence be assumed because their affairs are not entered in the Massachusetts Records. There was no reason why the business so unreservedly placed in the hands of the ten Undertakers, should appear in the records of affairs of the Colony, for all the Planters' interests had passed to their representatives among the Undertakers, but there is even a very good reason for such omission as it appears that the colonial Government utterly repudiated liability for the repayment of sums expended on their behalf. In 1647, the widow of Matthew Cradock, then married to Richard Glover, presented a claim for 679^{li} 6^s 4^d "disbursed for the country," which was again preferred three years later as "long since disbursed by herself or husband." After a careful scrutiny of the accounts, the Court, on 15 October, 1650, declared that both the receipts and disbursements concerned "only particular persons, or company of merchants, or undertakers and not the government now established, or people in general, who were never concerned therein nor had any such engagement upon them as the account mentions, and therefore not responsible for the debt demanded, as may appear in the Court book by several orders about transference of the government and managing of the joint stock, which was sold to particular persons upon their own account, as by said book of orders may appear in the 9th mo. 1629," [2] they therefore refused

2 *Massachusetts Records*, II, 226; III, 213.

to pay the sum demanded. Later, 6 May, 1658, the widow Cradock-Glover, having now married Dr. Whichcote, made a similar petition which was answered by a reference to the previous entry.[3]

In the Court book at the date named—the period dealt with just above—nothing is said about an actual sale of the Joint Stock to the Undertakers; it was valued and placed in their hands to be managed and afterwards they were to divide the capital and profits among the Adventurers. The entry is especially interesting as it refers to "particular persons, or company of merchants, or undertakers;" it looks as if these were three separate bodies: the "particular persons" may be the "Governor and his partners" who sent out "on their particular;" the "company of merchants" may be those whom Johnson hoped to "go securely on with;" and the "undertakers" would be the ten representatives so styled, and Cradock had disbursed money on behalf of all three. Furthermore, this entry proves the inaccuracy of the statement by W. R. Scott that the Joint Stock was to be divided among the colonists and the governor and deputy were to take over on their behalf the immovable property.[4]

It is quite evident then that the Undertakers' accounts were kept entirely separate from those of the colony and would not be entered in their records, and their ledgers have yet to be discovered. Still, the Massachusetts Records give a few hints of the existence of the English Adventurers and show that some action was taken by

[3] *Ibid.*, IV, p. 297.
[4] See above, p. 89, note.

them in connexion with the stocks under the control of the
Undertakers in the year 1634.

At that time Winthrop and Dudley were the only
Undertakers remaining in New England and the latter
was elected governor in the place of Winthrop at the General Court held on 1 May of that year—the first occasion
on which the secret ballot was used. An entry in the
Minutes of this Court reads: "The Deputy Governor
[Roger Ludlowe], Mr. Israel Stoughton and Mr. Coxeall
are desired by the Court to take an account of John
Winthrop, Esq. for such commodities as he hath received
of the Common Stock," [5] that is, the newly formed fund
for charitable and other benefits of the plantation,
founded on 10 February, 1629/30,[6] which is not to be
confounded with the earlier Common Stock. Taken in
conjunction with an entry made in the next Court it is a
plausible suggestion that some communication had been
received from England upon this subject. At this next
Court Winthrop's account was presented and the following entries occur: " . . . ordered, that the declaratory
account of John Winthrop, Esq., now exhibited into
Court shall be recorded," and " . . . ordered, that there
shall be letters written to these gentlemen hereunder mentioned and signed by the Court of Assistants, viz., Mr.
George Harwood, Mr. John Revell, Mr. Thomas Andrewes,
Mr. Richard Andrewes, Mr. Frauncis Kirby, Mr. Frauncis
Webb, Mr. George Foxcroft and Mr. Robert Keane, etc.
to entreat them to make choice of a man amongst ther

5 *Ibid.*, I, p. 120.
6 See above, p. 93.

selves to be Treasurer for a year, for the plantation, and also to give them power to receive an account of Mr. Harwood, now Treasurer, as also to give the said Mr. Harwood a full discharge." [7]

Referring to Winthrop's account we find it deals with "such things as I have received and disbursed for public use in the time of my government," and he states that he never received moneys or goods committed to him in trust for the Commonwealth other than those mentioned. He enumerates drumheads, powder, meal, rugs, suits, etc., and for money he accounts for 300^{li} disbursed in public services and another sum for Mr. Phillips and his family until he obtained a particular congregation. He explains that his office of Governor had been very costly and concludes "with this one request (which in justice may not be denied me) that as it stands upon record that upon the discharge of my office, I was called to account, so this my declaration may be also recorded; lest hereafter, when I shall be forgotten, some blemish may lie upon my posterity, when there shall be nothing to clear it." [8]

A plausible explanation of the situation may be that on the death, in 1633, of Aldersey, treasurer of the Joint Stock, Harwood had acted as treasurer *pro tempore*, and that a letter had been written by certain of the English Adventurers—and it should be noted that the only Undertaker who signed it was Revell, the first name after the treasurer's—to ask for the nomination of a treasurer and

---

[7] *Ibid.*, p. 128. The suggestion that this was a committee appointed by the Government in New England is improbable as care would have been taken to insert every name in the list and not leave any to be covered by "etc." There is evidence that all, except in the case of Kirby, subscribed to one of the above stocks.

[8] *Ibid.*, p. 132.

the acceptance of the temporary treasurer's account. To this may have been added a request for a statement of the disbursements made on the plantation, which naturally would have been required from Winthrop, the senior of the surviving Undertakers in New England. It will be seen that he accounts for munitions, food and clothing distributed to the necessitous and money expended for a minister—all matters that were to be paid for out of the fund styled the "Common Stock" in Harwood's hands by warrant from three Undertakers. Winthrop considered that a wrong interpretation might be placed upon the request, coming as it did, just as he was relieved of office—probably he was annoyed at his supercession by the other surviving Undertaker as well as at being treated like any ordinary trustee and required to give an account of his stewardship.[9]

It was near about the time of the expiration of the seven-years period that we find another entry suggesting that the affairs of the Joint Stock, in accordance with the agreement, were being wound up and this is followed by other significant entries.

On 6 September, 1638, the Minutes record that "Letters were appointed to be written to Mr. George Harwood, to desire him to send his account;" this must refer to the business of which we know he was acting as Treasurer. At the same Court a committee was appointed to consider the allowance of land and the names of such as

[9] On the other hand Robert C. Winthrop holds that this request shows "a salutary example of the strictness of our New England Fathers in holding even the most honoured of their rulers to account for the exercise of their authority and for the care of the public property." [*Life of Winthrop*, II, p. 123]

they find fit to receive land and the quantities to be allowed them "having regard to their adventures in the Common or Joint Stock, and their abilities to improve lands," as well as other allotments of land. They were reminded that "though the first planters were allowed fifty acres for each person yet this benefit is not to be allowed to all others." [10]

To certain persons known to have been Adventurers grants were made that same day but entered before the above order; on 3 June, apparently drawn up in compliance with that order, another list is given; after several names the services rewarded are specified and as the rest are for the most part known to have been Adventurers the remaining persons may have been in that category—thirteen in all—one allotment was made to "Tod for Mr. Young," and Richard Young, an Adventurer, is named in another entry relating to this grant.

In the same year two grants were made—in consideration of Mrs. Ann Harvey's 25^{li} and Edward Cooke's 100^{li} adventured in the *Joint Stock*. Possibly two more, Thomas Marsh and Joseph Hills, were also holders of Joint Stock as their allotments were "in respect of 33^{li} 6^s 8^d, according to the proportion agreed on for such adventure," which looks like the third part of 100^{li} subscribed but "drawn down" to one-third.[11]

Wade and Venn, whose sons claimed, had adventured in the *Country Stock*, which appears to have been identical with the *Common Stock* in which the remainder of the adventures are said to have been.

[10] *Massachusetts Records*, I, p. 240.
[11] See above, p. 87.

A curious entry, having perhaps a special meaning, is that relating to Sir Richard Saltonstall's allotment—he was to have the same as "other adventurers or *under-takers;*" as he obtained 1000 acres and as Winthrop and Dudley had the same, a special grant may have been made to undertakers, perhaps in lieu of the 5 per cent on profits which was to be paid them for their labours.[12]

In 1656 the executors of Isaac Johnson applied for a grant of 4200 acres for 400[li] subscribed to the Common Stock as nothing had been received on this acount "in the first divident." [13]

In only one case is there a hint that an Adventurer took out his adventure in cash. John Pocock, elected an Assistant 13 May, 1629, remained in England and from time to time transacted business for the Government in New England, occasionally acting as its agent. In 1651, among other moneys due to him the Court found it was "debtor to Mr. Pocock in England, for the sum of fifty pounds, formerly disbursed for and towards the use and benefit of the country." This amount was that usually subscribed and is "even figures" so it seems probable that it was his adventure in the early days.[14]

Certain persons are said to have subscribed to the Common Stock, e.g., in 1653 it is entered that Cole adventured fifty pounds "in the common stock twenty-three years since;" that is in the fund so styled of which Harwood was appointed treasurer on 10 February, 1629/30. This is a particularly interesting instance as my friend

---

[12] See above, p. 87.
[13] Elsewhere it is given as 3200 and was not to be granted until 10li due from the estate had been paid to the country treasurer.
[14] *Massachusetts Records,* IV, p. 74.

Colonel C. E. Banks informs me he found record of a law-suit between John Cole, of Clipsham, Co. Rutland,[15] and Thomas Goffe from which it appears that Cole subscribed 50^{li} to the Massachusetts Bay Company and had obtained no return for it. Goffe replied that the money was paid to Theophilus Eaton, who went to New England "about a year since," taking all the Company's books with him and that Mr. Harwood, formerly treasurer, had left the Company. Bearing in mind that the objects for which friends in England were asked to subscribe included munitions, fortifications, etc., it is probable that a couple of entries in the records in 1644 refer to this stock.

Stephen Winthrop had just obtained leave to sail for England when on 13 November, 1644, it was noted that there was "by account, 63^{li} 8^s 9^d in the hands of Mr. Edward Tynge, & 248^{li} in the hands of Captain Stoughton of the country's stock," [16] which the surveyor of arms was empowered to collect or recover by legal process; 100^{li} was to be paid to Mr. Rainborrowe and 100^{li} to Mr. Pocock; the balance, 111^{li} 8^s 9^d, was to be expended by Stephen Winthrop on musket bullets, lead and powder.[17]

One further reference to this Stock is found in the Massachusetts Records on 23 May, 1655: "There being information given to this Court that whereas there hath been formerly some gratuities given to this colony by some that have been well wishers to this country in England, and that there is yet remaining some part of the same undisposed of, it is ordered that Mr. Joseph Metcalf and Mr. George Gittings be authorized to enquire

15 Isaac Johnson came from Clipsham.
16 See above on the identity of the two stocks.
17 *Ibid.*, II, p. 82.

into this business, and to find out what may be due to this country in this or any other way, and the deputies of every town to enquire." [18] The first part of this entry appears to deal with the balance of the Common Stock still remaining undisposed of while the instructions to the deputies were probably added because it was known that several legacies had been left to the colony by residents in New England as well as England, which had not been paid in.

In view of these entries it can only be concluded that at the end of seven years from the date of the agreement a "divident" was made of lands to those who had adventured in the Joint Stock and that about the same time allotments, as promised, began to be made to the contributors to the Common Stock; these were continued over a dozen years or so; claims came in from England from time to time and were closely scrutinized, sometimes authority from an Adventurer to his son was not forthcoming; occasionally evidence of claim was not sufficient, a remarkable instance being that of Christopher Coulson, elected an Assistant on 13 May, 1629; the Court was not satisfied that the sum had been paid, or that his nephew had authority to receive the land.[19] There was great delay in the selection and survey of sites, sometimes due to an Adventurer desiring land in a particular district or because they had to search for land "which is not already allotted," with the result that the business dragged on— it is believed that the last claim was considered in 1660; as far as the Records go there is silence regarding the

18 *Ibid.*, IV, p. 223.
19 *Ibid.*, IV, p. 429.

English Adventurers and their treasurer, Harwood, but it is fairly safe to assume that their missing ledgers were finally closed about 1639. But one application, at least, was made after the settlement of their share of the business. Among the *Winthrop Papers* is a document endorsed by Winthrop himself "Copy of Mr. Spensers [and Cranes?] letter." [20] It is addressed to "the Governor & Assistance of the Plantation of New England in Matathucets Bay" and, after reference to the Court of the New England Company held on 31 November, 1629, when the Undertakers undertook to manage the Stock, it states that the undersigned, apparently more than one but their names are not given, in the time when Cradock was Governor had ventured in the Company 25^{li}, which was to be repaid in six months. They had demanded the money of "the Undertakers here" who had undertaken the whole stock of the Company [i.e. the New England Company], and had promised to pay all debts, some of which had been paid. The Undertakers answered that all had been paid out "as far as they received and put us over to Mr. John Wentrop, who was chosen presently after to be Governor, who oweth 100^{li} to the Company, out of which they say our money must be paid." As they had freely lent the money for the benefit of the Plantation, the prosperity of which they desired, they requested repayment of these debts that it might not redound to its dishonour. They awaited a favourable reply, but failing that they would commence a suit for recovery. In a postscript they say: "We forbear to speak of that agreement which was made when it was ordered by the Court, and condescended unto by the Undertakers, that the Joint Stock being brought into a 3^d part of what was put in, should be employed for seven years and the produce divided, I say, or that if any would take out his $\frac{1}{3}^d$ part of his Stock, he might have it, but we can get neither one nor the other."

A footnote in the *Winthrop Papers* suggests that this was from Mr. William Spencer, who in 1636, as the reference shows, was on a Committee to investigate the debts to and from the country when a new treasurer came into office. As this letter was evidently written from England it is quite probably from John Spencer, who went to New England in 1634 and later settled in Newbury. As he was one of those condemned in 1637 for signing a petition in favour of Wheelwright and Anne Hutchinson he returned to England, according to Savage, in the following year.[21]

In retaliation for his treatment it would have been natural for him to persuade other Old Adventurers to claim repayment of their investments from the English Undertakers; as their books were closed, as suggested above, about 1639, the applicants were referred to Winthrop who still owed one hundred pounds to the Company.

[21] Pope, *Pioneers of Massachusetts,* gives "Testimony regarding his business, Ips. Dec. 1, 38." This probably refers to the settlement of his affairs about the time he left.

XII

FREEMEN IN NEW ENGLAND

THE story of the Massachusetts Bay Company while it continued as a governing body in England is now completed but during the seven years period after the transfer of the government certain events occurred in the colony which are worth describing here because of their connexion with the Charter and the interpretation placed upon it after the Government had shaken off the restraining hand of the English Adventurers.

Reference has already been made to the lack of information concerning the freemen of the Company in England but there is much to be said about the freemen in New England and their struggle during the early years of the colony for the rights conferred by the Charter,— a struggle which resulted in a great constitutional change. At first these freemen were no more than freemen of a great livery company but, as will be seen, later they obtained a political status akin to that of freemen of a city—they ceased to take an oath to the Company and an oath to the Commonwealth was substituted.

Winthrop, the guiding spirit among the rulers in New England, must have conceived of the first freemen as *automata* intended to register approval of such matters as the authorities chose to lay before them, simply as a matter of form, without power to deal with taxation or legisla-

tion and but a limited power of election—the Charter
could not have meant what it distinctly said, was obviously
the opinion of the Governor, an aristocrat who had been
chosen "not by the multitude but by all the men of best
account among them." [1] It was only by degrees that the
popular voice wrung from him one concession after
another until their rights under the Charter were secured.

To understand the position it must be remembered that
the Charter ordered four General Courts to be held
annually. At that held on the last Wednesday of Easter
Term the majority of a duly constituted Court, consisting of the Governor, Deputy Governor, at least six Assistants and *such freemen as were present*, were to elect and
choose *out of the freemen* all the above officials annually. [2]

Immediately upon the arrival of Winthrop's party in
New England an attempt was made to contravene these
explicit instructions and to abolish the rights of the freemen before any in the colony were admitted.

At the first General Court, on 19 October, 1630, there
were present: the Governor, Deputy Governor, and six
Assistants; no freemen, according to Winthrop, except
the above existed on the plantation. It was propounded
that the best course would be for the freemen to choose
Assistants *when they are to be chosen*, and the Assistants,
from among themselves, to choose the Governor and
Deputy Governor—thus depriving the freemen of their
right to select the Governor *from among themselves*. To
this "the people," non-existent in the eye of the Charter,
assented by erection of hands. [3]

1 *Planters Plea*, p. 35.
2 *Massachusetts Records*, I, p. 10.
3 *Ibid.*, p. 79.

To avoid the necessity of choosing Assistants, the Court of Assistants held on 8 March following, ordered that if less than nine of their body were resident on the Plantation, the majority of those resident, i.e., five or *less* should constitute a quorum "as if there were the full number of seven," [4] pointedly recognizing the breach of the Charter. In consequence of this no Assistants were elected to fill vacancies until after the constitutional changes in 1634, to be dealt with presently, nor were they elected annually as the Charter required.

But these autocratic methods received a check. The constitution of the first General Court had precluded any protest against the proposal of the governing body for no one had any standing enabling them to make one,[5] but a different situation arose when the freemen were admitted in the following May. It must have been in deference to some objection from them that Winthrop, as the minutes inform us specifically, was chosen Governor "by the General consent of the Court, *according to the meaning of the patent*," [6] and that the order of the previous Court was *explained away*, for it was agreed that at the annual General Court the Commons, a body now first mentioned, should choose and elect Assistants and for "defect or misdemeanour" might remove the same.

But an ominous rider was added: in order that the

---

[4] *Ibid.*, p. 84.

[5] Savage notes the supineness of the people at the first Court, no jealousy was excited by the Governor and Assistants assuming legislative as well as executive and judicial powers, so he concluded the grant was not viewed as very important! His other remarks in the note should be compared with what is written below. [See Winthrop, *History*, I, p. 71, note.]

[6] *Massachusetts Records*, I, p. 87.

body of the Commons may be preserved "of honest and good men . . . no man shall be admitted to the freedom of this body politic but such as are members of some of the churches within the limits of the same." Here the word "Commons" appears to be synonymous with "freemen,"—for it was by the election of church-members that the freemen were to continue as a body of honest and good men.

And here must be considered the subject of the admissions to the freedom of the Company made at this time— a point of great importance for it has been so frequently stated that *from the outset* the above restriction was enforced, whereas such was by no means the case—yet arguments have been based upon this misstatement.[7] Blackstone, Maverick and several others who had not joined any local church then, or at a later date even, applied at the first Court, 19 October, 1630, and were not denied admission as freemen. An analysis of the list of those who applied for freedom at that Court shows that half the number were already in New England when Winthrop arrived,[8] it even seems probable that not only the advan-

---

[7] Osgood, *American Colonies*, I, p. 155, states that the authorities hesitated but *when the franchise had been limited to Church-members* freemen were admitted. Other writers have expressed the same more strongly.

[8] In this computation of the old settlers are included the company that sailed from Plymouth, West-countrymen, whose sympathies were with the Nahum Keike settlers, as well as those who had already settled at the latter place. Of those who applied but did not take up their freedom eight were old settlers and eight survivors of the new-comers, two military men and the beadle—the oaths of the last three would have covered that of the freemen. The two Normans, Walter Knight, the two Grays and Walford did not apply; the harsh treatment, quite probably deserved to some extent, meted out to some of these was due doubtless to the fact that they were not privileged freemen.

tages of becoming freemen were strongly urged but that some threats of dispossession may have been used against the reluctant, as we find some who were not freemen were punished by banishment. It is probable that Winthrop used every effort to bring all residents under the control of the Company, binding them to its service by an oath.[9]

Contrary to the requirements of the Charter no General Court was held until a year later, 9 May, 1632, and the first business then recorded is the reversal of the previous order relating to elections; the entry reads: "It was generally agreed upon, by erection of hands, that the Governor, Deputy Governor, and Assistants should be chosen by the whole Court of Governor, Deputy Governor, Assistants and freemen, and the Governor shall always be chosen out of the Assistants." And the statement that the Governor was elected by the general consent of the whole Court, manifested by the erection of hands, but without the reference to the Patent, is also made.

But before that Court met an incident had occurred which had an important bearing upon the constitution of the governing body. Early in February, 1631/2,[10] "the pastor and elder, etc." of Watertown had assembled the townspeople and publicly declared that they and their descendants would be slaves if they submitted to a levy made without their consent—so early arose the cry of "taxation without representation;" they declared the gov-

[9] The oath of freemen to the Company is found in *Massachusetts Records*, I, p. 353. The oath to the Commonwealth is on the following page.

[10] The date is fixed approximately by the fact that the levy was sanctioned on 3 February and Winthrop's meeting with the mutineers was on the 17th.

ernment "to be no other but a mayor and aldermen, who had no power to make laws or raise taxation without the people." Winthrop, having summoned the delinquents, by warrant or by letter, to answer for their mutinous conduct, persuaded them, for the moment, that the "government was rather in the nature of a parliament," that the concession of the previous year enabled them to elect or remove Assistants, and that at the General Court they had "free liberty to consider and propound anything concerning the same and to declare their grievances." [11]

The suggested analogy to a Parliament seems to have been pressed by the Watertown men and their sympathizers at the next General Court, for one of their objections was met by the appointment of a representative committee to consider taxation. This Committee has frequently been stated to have been the origin of the legislative assembly of the State. In Prince's *Chronology*, below the statement that the Committee was appointed, is a paragraph in brackets: "And this seems to pave the way for a House of Representatives in the General Court." [12] Savage, in a note to Winthrop's *History of New England* quotes Prince and gives the names of those who "formed this embryo of a parliament." [13] This idea has been elaborated by subsequent writers, it being asserted positively that the House of Representatives came into existence on that occasion.

The words of the Minutes of 9 May, 1632, do not war-

[11] *History of New England*, I, p. 71. Winthrop appears to insinuate that the freemen had delegated their authority to the Assistants, thus making them the authorized representatives of the people.

[12] *Op. cit.*, II, p. 60.

[13] *Op. cit.*, I, p. 76, note.

rant this conclusion; they read: "It was ordered that there should be two from every plantation appointed to confer with the Court about the raising of a public stock." The names immediately follow. Winthrop states the matter slightly differently. "Every town to choose two men to be at the next court, to advise with the Governor and assistants about the raising of a public stock, so as what they should agree upon should bind all, etc." [14]

The Committee was to consult with the rulers upon a particular question connected with the public stock and upon that occasion only, in fact they were a "consultative committee" in modern parlance; objection had been made to the imposition of a tax and a public stock was to be raised in some way and these representatives would no doubt be asked to apportion the sum for each plantation. Nothing in the way of legislative business was to be considered by them and when they had consulted with the ruling power their task was ended. They could have had no control over the imposition of taxation, otherwise Winthrop would not have suggested in 1634 as a concession that "no assessment should be laid upon the country without the consent of" a committee which he *then* proposed should be formed and be summoned at his pleasure. Nor could these sixteen men have formed a legislative assembly, as is so positively asserted by some writers, for Winthrop said at his interview with the Stoughton faction, that the freemen were so numerous that "it was not possible for them to make or execute laws, but they must choose others for that purpose; and that howsoever it would be necessary *hereafter* to have a select company to

[14] *Ibid.,* p. 76.

intend that work, yet for the present they were not furnished with a sufficient number of men qualified for such
a business." [15]

As a matter of fact two years elapsed before the legislative assembly was brought forth with many pangs—but
of that presently.

Just prior to the meeting of 9 May, at which the committee of sixteen was appointed, Winthrop entered in his
journal a curious statement. After a heated controversy
between himself and Dudley, of which we have his version
only, a peace was patched up and the assembled Assistants
adjourned to the dinner he had provided. Afterwards
Winthrop told them of a rumour "that the people
intended, at the next general court, to desire that the
Assistants ought to be chosen anew every year and that
the Governor might be chosen by the whole Court and not
by the Assistants only." This suggestion infuriated Ludlowe who maintained that there would be an interim when
men might do as they pleased.[16] Yet it was in strict
accord with the Charter.

Dealing with the Court held a week later, Winthrop
writes: "Whereas it was (at our first coming) agreed
that the freemen should choose the Assistants and they
the Governor, the whole Court agreed now, that the Governor and Assistants should all be new chosen every year
by the General Court (the Governor to be always chosen
out of the Assistants)." [17]

From the above it appears that the freemen on this
occasion regained some of the rights conferred by the

15 *Ibid.*, p. 128.
16 *Ibid.*, p. 74.
17 *Ibid.*, p. 75.

patent but not that of choosing the governor from among themselves.[18]   As this election was, however, made by a duly constituted General Court the anomalous position held by Winthrop hitherto was now changed; moreover, he was no longer a mere factor or agent appointed by a board of directors or Adventurers, as Conant and Endecott had been before him, but the political governor of a commonwealth, having, with his council, juridical and executive powers, being duly elected by the body of freemen.

The reluctance shown by Winthrop in allowing the freemen the rights and privileges bestowed upon them by the Charter is remarkable but two points had now been gained —the right to take part in the governor's election and that of being consulted in regard to the incidence of taxation. The movement, encouraged by this success, was increasing in volume and voice; when the opportunity arrived in 1634 a spokesman also appeared to advance the cause of liberty.   He has himself recorded the course of events so we are not wholly dependent upon Winthrop's account.

[18] Winthrop's statements make the entry in the minutes of the General Court of 18 May, 1631, very puzzling; there it is stated that the Governor [but not the other officers] was chosen "by the general consent of the Court according to the meaning of the patent," while the election was now to be made "by the whole court and not by the assistants only." This indicates that the previous election had been made by the assistants alone; if so, where in the patent could he find authority for such an election?   The patent defines the Company as consisting of the named officials and the freemen to be hereafter admitted and the elections were to be "by such greater part of the *Company*" then present.   A suggested explanation is that the new freemen had not at the moment of the election been sworn and the governing members being *ex officio* freemen it was considered that they by themselves constituted a court within the meaning of the patent.   It is somewhat significant that the order instituting the change made in 1632 defines the *whole court* as composed of Governor, Deputy Governor, Assistants *and freemen.*

XIII

STOUGHTON AND EFFORTS FOR LIBERTY

ISRAEL STOUGHTON, the brother of a somewhat famous Puritan divine in London, emigrated to New England in 1630 accompanied by his brother Thomas. He states that on his arrival and for a whole year thereafter he found that the government "was solely in the hands of the assistants, the people chose them magistrates, and then they made laws, disposed lands, raised monies, punisht offenders, etc. at their discretion; neither did the people know the pattent nor what prerogatives and liberty they had by the same. But there being some sums of money asked and a speech of more, it made some inquisitive into matters and particularly after the pattent; about which time Mr. Wenthrop Governor having the pattent did give way to the country upon their motion to see it." [1]

Winthrop's account so far is substantially the same; he says that after the issue of notices of the General Court to be held on the 14 May, 1634, "the freemen deputed two of each town to meet and consider of such matters as they were to take order in at the same General Court;

[1] This and the following quotations are from Stoughton's letter, *State Papers, Colonial,* VIII, No. 16. I brought this to the notice of the *Massachusetts Historical Society* and it was printed in the Proceedings, LVIII, p. 446, with an introductory note by myself. I have since collated the transcript there given with the original MS. making the necessary corrections.

who, having met, desired a sight of the patent, and conceiving thereby that all their laws should be made at a General Court, repaired to the Governor to advise with him about it and about the abrogating of some orders formerly made, as for killing of swine in corn, etc." He excused the arbitrary course heretofore followed by saying that "when the patent was granted the number of freemen was supposed to be (as in like corporations) so few, as they might well join in making laws; but now they were grown to so great a body, as it was not possible for them to make or execute laws, but that they must chose others for that purpose; and that howsoever it would be necessary hereafter to have a select company to intend that work, yet for the present they were not furnished with a sufficient number of men qualified for such a business, neither could the commonwealth bear the loss of time of so many as must intend it. Yet this they might do at present, viz. they might at the general court, make an order, that once in the year, a certain number should be appointed (upon summons from the governor) to revise all laws, etc. and to reform what they found amiss therein; but not to make any new laws, but prefer their grievances to the court of assistants; and that no assessment should be laid upon the country without the consent of such a committee, nor any lands disposed of." [2]

From this it appears that not only no deputies of freemen had yet been appointed but that the committee which was to be called *when it pleased the Governor*, was to have but limited powers; beyond this he was not prepared to relax his arbitrary rule. Commenting upon this, J. T.

[2] Winthrop, *History of New England*, I, p. 128. The number of freemen admitted to this date was 220, but a considerable number had died.

Adams writes, "It is difficult to conceive of a more complete abrogation of the rights of even the very limited body of freemen." [3]

However, Stoughton informs us that "all the Magistrates (as in charitie I must say), were willing to admitt the people to joyne with themselves in the governance of the state, by three deputies from each towne." Here he must be excluding the Governor from the term "magistrates" and it may be noted that he makes no reference to the limitation of the power of the proposed deputies suggested by Winthrop.

When the next General Court assembled on 14 May, 1634, three deputies were appointed from each town—a single deputy is by Stoughton styled a "comity" and Stoughton was chosen a "comity" for the town of Dorchester; and by the Committees he was "chosen the chief speaker on the country's behalf (there being 3 speakers) and indeed such was their good opinion of me (unworthy I confess) that they would have chose me into an assistant's place but they said they needed me more there for the present." At this Court, which lasted three days, "many good orders were made," as the Minutes show. They instituted a new freemen's oath in which they refer to "this common weale" [4] and its government and after this declared what were the powers belonging

[3] *Founding of New England*, p. 160.
[4] The earlier oath declares that the freeman has become "a member of this body, consisting of the Governor, Deputy Governor, Assistants, & a commonalty of the Mattachusetts in New England." This appears to have been the oath administered in 1631. Osgood says, *American Colonies*, I, p. 155, that the 1634 oath "took the place of an earlier one which apparently has not been preserved. If by the reference is meant an oath administered to members of the corporation while resident in England, the nature of the two is wholly different." The two oaths are given in *Massachusetts Records*, I, pp. 353, 354.

to the General Court as a legislative and executive body —there should be no trial for life or for banishment without a jury summoned; there should be four courts yearly and these should not be dissolved without the consent of the majority of the Court; they repealed the obnoxious laws regarding swine and, with astounding courage, they set a fine for a breach of an order "against imployeing Indeans to shoote with peeces," upon Mr. Mayhew as well as upon the previous Court of Assistants who gave him leave. An order was also drawn up concerning the choosing by the freemen of each plantation of "two or three" from each town with their duties clearly laid down.[5]

In such manner was carried through the great constitutional change that finally transformed the trading company into a political state, with its legislative and executive duties clearly defined. On this occasion, when the new oath was sanctioned and taken, the Commonwealth of Massachusetts came into existence with its duly constituted legislature.

One of the most important changes was the introduction of the secret ballot—for the first time the Governor was elected "by papers,"—an event relegated by Winthrop to a marginal note. The result was remarkable, for instead of the re-election of Winthrop, Dudley was chosen Governor and Ludlowe Deputy Governor—a strange effect of the first free election in the colony and the more remarkable because Winthrop and Dudley had, as we have seen, but recently been reconciled after a serious quarrel.

There were several reasons for this deposition of Win-

5 *Massachusetts Records*, I, p. 117, *et seq.*

throp, but chief among them was the dissatisfaction felt
because of his arbitrary methods, voiced by Stoughton
and his party, who felt much resentment at the treatment
to which they had been subjected. This was aggravated
by a sermon preached on the day of the election by John
Cotton, newly arrived in the country, in which he "delivered the doctrine that a magistrate ought not to be
turned into the condition of a private man without just
cause, and to be publickly convict," i.e., by charges
brought and proved in a public meeting.

Stoughton comments upon the proceedings of this
Court that "tho' there was a little opposition in our particular case, yet all ended in peace with manifestations
of great love and the magistrates good approbation of
us that had in some points opposed and crost them."
Winthrop's account is that "all things were carried peace-
ably, notwithstanding that some of the assistants were
questioned, and some fines imposed but remitted before
the Court brake up . . . the new governor and the
assistants were together entertained at the house of the
old governor as before." [6] The canny Puritan could not in
conscience waste the baked meats provided to celebrate
Winthrop's triumph!

These two narratives supplement each other and set
clearly before us the manner in which the change in the
method of governing the Colony took place; it enables
us to correct certain errors heretofore accepted by historians. Savage would have us believe that "the assistants were become weary of the exercise of all the powers

---

[6] See above for the fining of the assistants; a marginal note states
that the fine was remitted.

of government, and desired others to participate in the responsibility." [7]   No surmise could be much further from the truth.   Those in authority, seeking to rule as *they* thought best for the inhabitants, found themselves confronted by opponents equally resolute to establish the charter rights of the freemen, which were finally reluctantly granted.   It was not, therefore, by the gracious gift of the weary ruling powers but after a severe struggle, having many untoward effects, that true Liberty, as guaranteed by the Charter, was obtained.

[7] Wintĥrop, *History of New England,* I, p. 129, note.

XIV

LIBERTY TRIUMPHANT

STOUGHTON provides some interesting comments on the election which took place on 14 May, 1634. He writes to his friends at home: "To tell you the truth (for it is like you may hear it from others) Mr. Winthrop had very many hands against him for being either governor (which some attempted) or assistant. The cause, it is like they know best that put in blanks. I suppose they were not his enemies, nor none of the most simple. He hath lost much of that applause that he hath had (for indeed he was highly magnified) and I hear some say they put in blanks, not simply because they would not have him magistrate, but because they would admonish him thereby to look a little more circumspectly to himself. He is indeed a man of men, but he is but a man and some say they have idolized him and do now confess their error. My opinion is that God will do him good by some, as also he hath done good to some by him; and that he is a godly man and a worthy magistrate notwithstanding some few passages at which some have stumbled." This expression of opinion was exceptionally noble as in the interval between the election and the penning of these lines Stoughton had had a very unpleasant experience of Winthrop's wrath which was unjustly wreaked upon him.

As it illustrates further Winthrop's arbitrary methods and his interpretation of the Charter a passing reference is made to it here.

Stoughton tells us that at a Court in August, 1634, at which he was both a "comitee & speaker (as before)" there were "some straight passages and specially about the negative voice, which fell to be my portion much to oppose, though not alone." On this occasion he and Winthrop had had some private discourse upon which the latter later relied for certain of his charges; for some of the straight passages Winthrop excused himself, so all ended well. At the next Court, in March following, Endecott's action in cutting the Cross from the flag was to be dealt with and it was believed that the question of "the negative voice" would also come up. For this reason Stoughton was asked to put in writing his contention concerning the latter point; at first he refused but was at last persuaded and wrote out his arguments hurriedly as time was short. Mr. Warham, his pastor, desired to read these and then, *without permission asked,* he handed them to Mr. Cotton, who finding something obscure, or so pretending, on the morning of the meeting handed the "book" to Winthrop—a most unwarrantable and pernicious proceeding.

Ignorant of the course of events, Stoughton attended the Court and Winthrop, in the presence of the Assistants, exclaimed, to use the somewhat mixed phraseology of Stoughton, "This is the man that had been the trobler of Israel and that I was a worme (such an one as Mr. Hooker has spoken of in his sermon) and an underminer of the faith and yet saith he, who but Mr. Stoughton in

the eie of the country, and saith he, I had from a speciall
friend (I suppose it was Dr. Wright)[1] a letter of good
report of me that I was a man worthy of his acquaintance but I had never come at him (wherein I confesse I
have been something fayling through shamefastness and
a natural defect that way, yet I have been with him
divers times and allwaies shewed him great respect, as all-
soe and in truth he has done to me above my deserts).
But now to the point. they charged my booke for this
and that. One thing was that I should say in it, that I
by my fact had freed the state so and so," [that is, he
had boasted that at the previous court he had obtained
the freemen's rights granted by the patent]. This he
denied and demanded to see the passage; he was obliged
to admit that "there wanted a comma but that being
added they [the Magistrates] all confessed the sense was
quite otherwise and so were cilenced in that point, and
it was so plain without the comma that no man excepted
at that till Mr. Winthrop nor did any make such sence
of it but he and such as he possest. But then the main
accusation which they stuck to was that I denyed the
Assistants to be Magistrates, and made them but Ministers of Justice." While affirming that he never denied
them to be magistrates he admitted that he had said they
were Ministers of Justice as well as Magistrates by the
rule of Romans, 13,2. and by the custom of London; he
pointed out that the "patent makes their power ministerial according to the greater voat of the general court

[1] Dr. Nathaniel Wright, with whom Winthrop corresponded, is
said to have been physician to Oliver Cromwell; he is not to be
confounded with the merchant and Assistant of that name. See
p. 161.

and not magisterial according to their decision," they could not do ought or hinder ought according to their own wills but they must respect General Courts "which by patent consist of the whole company of freemen." [2] The Assistants took offence at some other statements which were admittedly "very playne English," but they would not specify other charges than the two,—i.e. the sense without the comma and the ministerial powers. However, for the sake of peace Stoughton was willing that the "book" should be burnt, as he counted it of little importance, but neither Winthrop nor Ludlowe was satisfied with that and matters that were spoken in private were brought up against Stoughton while they refused to listen to anything in his defence, even his witnesses were denied a hearing. They demanded the public burning of his book and his disablement from office for three years, to which they persuaded the Court to agree. They were sufficiently spiteful to have it recorded that what Stoughton calls "the thing" "was burnt as weak and offencive." [3]

Winthrop's account declares that Stoughton asserted that the power of the Governor was ministerial; that he opposed the Magistrates, slighted them and used many weak arguments against the negative voice. Although Dorchester presented a petition against this sentence upon Stoughton at the next Court it was rejected "and the sentence affirmed by the country to be just," Winthrop states, adding this rider: "Divers jealousies, that

---

[2] In this he had certainly grasped the meaning of the patent correctly.

[3] *Massachusetts Records*, I, p. 135.

had been between the magistrates and deputies, were now cleared, with full satisfaction to all parties." [4]

But when Vane was elected Governor in place of Winthrop on 25 May, 1636, one of the first matters dealt with by the Court was the restoration of Stoughton to his former liberty, by removing the disqualifying sentence and enabling him to bear office, with the result that at the very first opportunity he was elected "by the country" to an Assistant's room,[5] where now it was counted that he could do more good than as deputy fighting for their cause.

So ended Stoughton's efforts to establish the freemen's rights conferred upon them by the Charter; here, as the New England emigrants had rebelled against Laud's arbitrary action in ecclesiastical affairs, these freeborn Englishmen in the colony rebelled against this encroachment upon their rights.

[4] *History of New England,* I, p. 160. In his dispute in 1632 with Dudley, Winthrop maintained that "the patent making him a governour gave him whatsoever power belonged to a governour by common law or the statutes," therefore his authority surpassed that of the Assistants. His prejudice against Stoughton, as against all who questioned his opinions, is evident, and he was not always scrupulously accurate in his statements. When calling attention to an inaccuracy or rather a misrepresentation of actual facts, in the Massachusetts Records, relating to Wheelwright, C. F. Adams expresses the pious hope that for Winthrop's credit he was not responsible for this perversion. Winthrop was "but a man" and allowed prejudice to colour many of his remarks to the detriment of accuracy.

[5] *Massachusetts Records,* I, p. 175.

XV

SUMMARY

THE story of the founding of Massachusetts has now been traced through its various stages.

The Dorchester Company, under the pioneer Roger Conant, lacking in experience, amid many trials, well and truly laid the foundation stones although their share has been to so large an extent overlooked. "Experience hath taught us that as in building houses the first stones of the foundation are buried underground and are not seen, so in planting colonies the first stones employed that way are consumed, although they serve for a foundation of the work." [1]

The New England Company, under the forceful Governor, John Endecott, took over the results of the experience and labours of the Dorchester men and added their share to the superstructure.

The Massachusetts Bay Company, under the aristocratic and autocratic John Winthrop, without proper acknowledgment of their predecessors' work, took possession of a colony ready to their hand and, after relaying certain faulty courses they had built in, and not without flaws, reared their portion of the stately structure now known as the Commonwealth of Massachusetts.

[1] *Planters Plea,* p. 42.

Each company did its part and to every man should be granted due recognition.

The material, meagre though it be, for the history of this period has been chronologically arranged, placed in proper perspective and strung together by inferences and conjectures which it is hoped will be found in every case legitimate, in order to make a clear story of the early work of laying the foundations of the Colony. If such inferences and conjectures do not meet with the acceptance of the reader, the material, with full reference to sources, will enable him to form his own judgment. If he can make a more correct use of that material he will do a service to the students of colonial history and earn the gratitude of the writer. To the careful and intelligent student she leaves the improvement of this labour of love.

XVI

ADVENTURERS IN THE MASSACHUSETTS BAY COMPANY

IN the following list of Adventurers I have included the seven ministers, five sent out by the Company and two admitted as chaplains in London, although there is no evidence that they subscribed for stocks, yet they attended meetings; also several who left legacies in such form as to suggest subscriptions, but all such are marked with § and the facts stated in the biographical sketch.

It is somewhat uncertain whether the sums given in Felt's second list are additional to those in the first or whether they represent deferred payments; the fact that two new names occur suggests that the former was the case.

Where the Adventurer is well known, e.g. Winthrop, Higginson, Dudley, I have omitted details, giving only notes connected with their subscription or the first mention of their presence at meetings of the Company, referring the reader to "the usual sources," i.e. books on early New England history, as Winthrop's *History of New England*, Hubbard, Savage's *Dictionary*, etc.

The "Impropriations Fund" mentioned several times was formed for the maintenance of Puritan Preachers in England, subscriptions thereto indicate interest in the

Puritan movement and that a common meeting ground of members of the Company would have been at the board of the Feoffees for Impropriations.

ABBREVIATIONS

E. Signer of Endecott's *Instructions,*   May, 1628
F. Felt's *Annals of Salem,* I, 508   May, 1628
FF. "   "   "   "   , 1, 509.
H. Haven's entries in *Massachusetts*
    Records omitted in Shurtleff.   30 March, 1629
Hub. Hubbard, *History of New England,* p. 123.
MR. *Massachusetts Records,* ed. Shurtleff.
Reg. *New England Historic-Genealogical Register.*

["John White" is my own book on "John White, the Founder of Massachusetts."]

—— ABRIE. Perhaps John Aubrey, of Cheapside, merchant, a subscriber to the Impropriations Fund.

THOMAS ADAMS of London, woollen-draper. Son of Thomas Adams of Wem, Salop, by Margaret, daughter of John Erpe of Shrewsbury. In 1647, when an alderman of London, he was sent to the Tower for treason to the Parliament. He married Anne, dau. Humfrey Mapled of Printon, Essex.

[He was probably the "cousin Thomas Adams the elder" mentioned in the will of Captain Adams in 1657.]

E. F. 50^{li}; FF. 25^{li}; MR. 50^{li}

SAMUEL ALDERSEY, of Allhallows, Lombard Street, haberdasher. Son of John Aldersey of Aldersey, Cheshire, by Anne, sister of Sir Thomas Lowe, Alderman of London. He married first, Mary, dau. Philip Van Oyrle of Nornberg and Antwerp; second, Margaret, dau. Thomas Offspring and sister of Rev. Charles Offspring of St. Antholins, London, widow of William Kedward. [She remarried Sir John Melton.] Aldersey was a prominent Puritan who contributed to the Impropriations Fund in 1626 and was probably an active worker for St. Antholin's Feoffees as his brother-in-law, Charles Offspring, was rector of that Church. He was an early Adventurer and took active part in the Company's work.

By the marriages of his sisters and of his children he was closely connected with a number of persons interested in the settlement of New England. His sister Elizabeth married 1st., William Pitchford and 2nd Sir Thomas Coventry, the Lord Keeper. Alice married Thomas Moulson and her son Sir Thomas was the husband of Anne Ratcliffe, the patron saint of Radcliffe College. Her daughter Rebecca married Nicholas Raynton, famous as a London Puritan. Another sister of Samuel married Francis Webbe; Mary married Sir Thomas Knatchbull and Dorothy, as her second husband married Sir Henry Capel. Still another sister seems to have married Henry Parkhurst as his son, Sir Robert, mentions his aunt Aldersey and nearly all the married Aldersey sisters in his will in 1636. As William Spurstowe married Sir Robert's sister he was in a way connected with Aldersey, as were also the Byfields.

Aldersey had one son, John, and four daughters; Mary married Robert Crane of St. Giles, Cripplegate [see below], Anne married Robert Eyre of Salisbury, son of Robert Eyre one of the Feoffees for Impropriations; Elizabeth married Thomas Lee of Downhall; Margaret married Rev. Thomas Bletchingdon, Canon of Christ Church, Canterbury.

Aldersey's will was proved 13 July, 1633 [P. C. C. 61 Russel], by Robert Crane and his son John Aldersey. By it he left £20 to Mr. Davenport, the minister; he had witnessed this minister's signing of the Articles in 1628.

E. F. 50^{li}; FF. 25^{li}; H. 75^{li}; MR. 50^{li}

RICHARD ANDREWES, of London, haberdasher and an Alderman. Perhaps resided in Cheapside as Winthrop addressed a letter to him at "the Mermaid" there. He was closely associated with the Plymouth Plantation. For particulars see above, pp. 8, 99.
He contributed to the Impropriations Fund in 1625.

THOMAS ANDREWES, of London, leather-seller. Son of Robert Andrewes of Feltham, Midds. He was Sheriff of London in 1642 and as Lord Mayor in 1649 proclaimed the abolition of kingly government. He was one of the Plymouth Adventurers who sold out their interests to the Planters in 1626 and probably was the one of that name who married Damaris Cradock.
He was present at a Company meeting on 6 April, 1629.

MR. 25^{li}

§ JOHN ARCHER ⎫ These two are frequently confused—see
　　　OR　　　 ⎬ 　　note in "John White;" most prob-
HENRY ARCHER ⎭ 　　ably this was Henry Archer who was incumbent of Allhallows, Lombard Street at this time. He was appointed Chaplain and admitted to the freedom of the Company on 20 November, 1629.

ANDREW ARNOLD.
Possibly a member of the Somerset family two of whom emigrated to New England.

F. 50^{li}; FF. 50^{li}

WILLIAM BACKHOUSE, of Swallowfield, Berks. Son of Samuel Backhouse of that place, and born about 1593. He "became a most renowned chymist, Rosicrucian, and a great encourager of those that studied chymistry and astrology, especially Elias Ashmole, whom he adopted as his son." He was the author of several books. He died 30 May, 1662. [Wood's *Athenæ*, III, 576.] He was

at a Company meeting on 5 April, 1629, and presented
a number of books including an English Bible in folio
of the last print; *The Booke of Common Prayer* [which
it was boasted was never used]; Calvin's *Institutes* and
The French Country Farm. [H.]

H. 25^{li}

DANIEL BALLARD. He was at a Company meeting on 17
April, 1629; in 1645 he was associated with John White,
probably the Counsellor, as receiving money from Sir
Richard Saltonstall, apparently in connexion with the
Quo Warranto.

F. 50^{li}; FF. 15^{li}; MR. 25^{li}

§ SIR NATHANIEL BARNARDISTON, of Ketton, Suffolk, knt.
Winthrop mentions his intention to become an Adventurer in 1630 [I, p. 355]. By his will, proved 28 September, 1653 [P. C. C. 376 Brent. (Reg. 48, 379)] he
left a legacy for the bringing up of [Indian ?] children
in the College of New England.

—— BATEMAN.
As "Mr. Bateman" he was at a meeting on 29 September, 1629. He may have been the Robert Bateman who
was interested in the Virginia Company [See Alexander
Browne's *Genesis of the United States*, p. 826], and who
was Chamberlain of London. This seems the more likely
because his wife was Joan Munser from Weymouth so
he may have known John White of Dorchester.

RICHARD BELLINGHAM.
An original Associate of the Patentees but took no active
part, apparently, while the Company held Courts in
England; he emigrated in 1634. See usual sources.

F. 50^{li}

—— BILSON.

As "Mr. Bilson" he was at a meeting on 21 May, 1629. Possibly he may have been the same as William Balston who emigrated.

JOHN BOWLES.

Possibly John Bolles of St. James, Clerkenwell, Middx., Esq., in whose will, proved 9 May, 1666 [P. C. C. 71 Mico. (Reg. 46, 336)], mention is made of his brother Joseph in New England.

H. 25li

JOB BRADSHAWE. Son of Joseph Bradshaw of Westminster, brewer, who contested that constituency in 1628 with Sir Robert Pye. Job was at a meeting on 20 October, 1629.

F. 50li; FF. 50li

JOSEPH BRADSHAWE, brother of the above.

His widow Elizabeth in her will, proved 27 April, 1658 [P. C. C. 137 Wootton], mentions his brothers Job and Abraham and his sons Joseph, Benjamin and John— Joseph being then out of England. He was at a meeting on 28 July, 1629. His will was proved 4 January, 1632/3 [P. C. C. 5 Russell].

F. 50li; FF. 50li

SIMON BRADSTREET.   See usual sources.

At a meeting on 23 March, 1629/30.

SIR WILLIAM BRERETON, knt. [of Malpas Hall, Cheshire.]

He was somewhat famous as a traveller in the Low Countries; he was a member of Parliament and is said to have been one of the judges of Charles I. He obtained a grant of land in Massachusetts from John Gorges and tried to induce the Company to give him an equivalent holding in their company; they refused, suggesting he might become an Adventurer in the usual way. Apparently he did so before 10 February, 1629/30, as on that day reference is made to 600 acres he was to have "by virtue of his Adventure in the Common Stock." [MR. I, pp. 28, 68]

§ FRANCIS BRIDGES, of Clapham, Surrey.

In his will proved 23 June, 1642 [P. C. C. 80 Cambell (Reg. 45, 162)], he left 50^{li} to the College in New England and 20^{li} towards clothing the poor there so it seems possible he subscribed 50^{li} to one of the Stocks. He was a cousin of Rev. Charles Offspring of St. Antholins and mentions Mr. Pemberton. He was one of the Feoffees for Impropriations.

§ FRANCIS BRIGHT, one of the ministers sent out by the Company. Son of Edward Bright of London; of New Inn Hall, Oxford, 1622. For further particulars see pp. 32–37.

JOHN BROWNE, of Roxwell, Essex, probably grandson of John Browne of Fidelers in Writtle, through one of his sons, Sir Henry, John, Charles or Edward, who were all living in 1612 [*Essex Visitation.*] For further information see above and in "John White."

KELLAM BROWNE, of Roxwell, Essex, probably a brother of the above. He signed the Cambridge Agreement [see p. 74] but did not emigrate. He married at St. Mary Aldermary, Mrs. Philip Filder of St. Saviours, Southwark. His will was proved 15 February, 1657/8 [P. C. C. 105 Wootton].

SAMUEL BROWNE, brother of John Browne above; see same sources.

—— BURNELL.

Possibly Thomas Burnell, of London, citizen and clothworker, son of John Burnell of Great Stanmore, Middx., for we find: (1) that the latter appointed as an over-

seer of his will, proved 23 January, 1622 [P. C. C. 7
Swann. (Reg. 46, 1551)], "the Right Worshipful and
my especial kind friend Sir Thomas Coventry, knight,"
that is the Lord Keeper, who was brother-in-law to both
this Burnell and to Samuel Aldersey; (2) that Thomas
in his will, proved 2 October, 1666 [P. C. C. 150, May
(Reg. 38, 419)], mentions his nephew John Morley in
New England, and (3) that his widow, Hester, in her
will, proved 15 October, 1664, [P. C. C. 109 Bruce (Reg.
48, 273)], mentions her cousins: John Crowther, Lucy,
wife of Clement Manistey, and [James] Yonge; so many
names associated with the Company, taken with other
references above, suggest that Thomas Burnell was the
Adventurer.

RICHARD BUSHROD, of Dorchester, Dorset, haberdasher.

For an account of this Adventurer see "John White."

F. 50^{li}

MRS. A. C. [OR MR.]

It is just possible that this was Anne Clement, widow of
John Clement of Shenfield, Essex, mentioned in a letter
from Augustine Clement, an emigrant, as his sister-in-
law, in 1638. He mentions a Mr. John Bateman, minister of Ockendon, who might be the —— Bateman above.
In Felt's list the name is Mr. A. C.; in Haven's it is
Mrs. A. C.

F. 50^{li}; FF. 50^{li}; H. 25^{li}

JOSEPH CARON, of London.

His name occurs in a list of members of the Skinners
Company in 1641, "his dwelling unknown." He may
have been a kinsman of Sir Noel de Caron, ambassador
from the Netherlands, who died at Lambeth in 1624.

E. F. 50^{li}; FF. 15^{li}; H. 25^{li}; MR. 25^{li}

—— CLARK.

He is simply "Mr. Clark" in the list of subscribers on
17 June, 1629, and the same day he was appointed

one of the eight auditors as "Mr. Clarke." These are the only instances found of the occurrences of his name. There was an Edward Clarke related to the Woodgate family [see below] but there is no means of identifying this Mr. Clark.

MR. 25^{li}

WILLIAM CODDINGTON.   See usual sources.

He was present on 23 March, 1629/30.

WILLIAM COLBRON, of Brentwood, Essex.

He emigrated with Winthrop. He was present 27 April, 1629. Pope, *Pioneers of Massachusetts*, says his receipt for 25^{li} stock is dated 8 May, 1629. On 26 May, 1658 he was granted 300 acres "where he can find it in refference to twenty-five pounds by him formerly paid into y^c common stock." [MR. IV, 336.]

SAMUEL COLE.

He emigrated with Winthrop. He was granted 400 acres in 1653 "in satisfaction of fifty pounds adventured in the common stock 23 years since." [MR. III, 147.]

EDWARD COOK, of London, apothecary. Son of Richard Cook of Dunmow, Essex. His second son, Robert, was granted 800 acres "where he can find it without prejudice to any plantation" for his father's 100^{li} adventured in the joint stock. [MR. I, 307.] Before 23 October, 1650, he re-granted this to Harvard College. [MR. III, 296.]

MR. 25^{li}

CHRISTOPHER COULSON.

He was present on 2 March, 1628/9, and, with John Pocock, was elected Assistant in place of Endecott and Browne on 13 May, 1629. [MR. I, 29, 40.] In 1660 his nephew Francis Johnson applied for a grant of land on account of Coulson's subscription but being unable to produce proof that it had been paid Johnson was refused. [MR. IV, 429.]

MATTHEW CRADOCK, of London, skinner. Son of Matthew Cradock of Stafford by Dorothy Greenham and brother of
Samuel Cradock of Thiselton, Rutland. He married 1st,
Damaris, daughter of Richard Wyn of Shrewsbury, by
whom he had Damaris, who married Thomas Andrewes
[See above.] 2nd, Rebecca, dau. Thomas Jordan of
London, merchant, by whom he had a son Matthew living in 1634, who probably died before his father as he
is not mentioned in the latter's will and his mother
Rebecca made no claim to Cradock's estate on her son's
behalf. There were many other Matthew Cradocks but
this one probably died young. Governor Cradock was a
member for Staffordshire in several Parliaments. In his
will, proved 4 June, 1641 [P. C. C. 81 Evelyn] we
read: "As for my outward estate wherewith God of
his goodness hath endowed me, I have ever accounted
myselfe but a steward thereof, and therfor humblie
intreat the Almightie to make me for to demeane myselfe
in the disposing thereof as that I might through his mercie
in the merits of Christ bee alwayes prepared to give a
comfortable accompt of my stewardshipp." He left
legacies to: St. Peter the Poor in Broad Street; to St.
Swithin "where I now dwell;" to his wife Rebecca and
her children; to her a house in London and another in
Romford, Essex, she to have during her natural life half
of his estate in New England; if she marry, her husband
to give bond and enjoy it during her life; the other half
to his daughter Damaris. His widow married Richard
Glover and after his death Benjamin Whichcote, son of
Christopher and brother of Charles Whichcote [See
below]. She appears to have been a widow when Cradock married her as he speaks of her children. For the
claims made by her and her husbands, see p. 97.

By his marriage with Damaris Wyn Cradock was connected with the Spurstowes, Alderseys, Parkhursts, Oldfields, Moulsons, etc.

E. F. 50^{li}; FF. 25^{li}; MR. 150^{li}; Hub. 100^{li}

Robert Crane, of St. Giles, Cripplegate, grocer. Son of
Robert Crane, of Great Coggeshall, Essex, grocer, and
brother of Margaret Crane, wife of Ezekiel Rogers,
therefore uncle of Mary Rogers, who married Rev. William Hubbard, the historian. Robert Crane married
Mary, daughter of Samuel Aldersey. He was present
13 May, 1629. His will was proved 21 September, 1646.
[P. C. C. 131 Twisse (Reg. 41, 177.)]

H. 25^{li}; Hub. 50^{li}

William Crowther, of St. Lawrence Jewry, haberdasher.
Son of John Crowther, of Shropshire, by his wife Margaret. He married Katherine, daughter of Richard Fox,
of London, merchant. He was present on 13 May, 1629.
In his will proved 29 May, 1658 [P. C. C. 249 Wootton],
he left many legacies to ministers, including the famous
Calamy, and gave instructions that "noe other banquet-
ting be used at my funeral but only Naples Biskett,
Mackeromes and Wine." [See reference to John Crowther in Hester Burnell's will above.]

F. 50^{li}; H. 25^{li}

William Darbie, of Dorchester, Dorset, mercer. See "John
White."

F. 50^{li}

John Davenport, minister. See usual sources.
He was present 23 March, 1628/9. He was a Feoffee
for Impropriations. In a letter, the reference to which
I have lost, he says he and Eaton subscribed 50^{li} each.

H. 25^{li}

Richard Davis, of London, merchant. Probably son of John
Davis of Denbigh by his wife Katherine, dau. William
Crooke, of Chilton, Bucks. He was one of the Feoffees
for Impropriations, and in the suit is described as a vintner. He was present on 17 June, 1629.

E. F. 50^{li}; H. 25^{li}

EMANUEL DOWNING, of the Inner Temple. See usual sources. His name has been added in brackets to a list of 15 October, 1629, but it seems doubtful whether he took any active part until after he emigrated.

THOMAS DUDLEY, agent to the Earl of Lincoln. See usual sources. He was present 15 October, 1629.

HENRY DURLEY, son of Sir Richard Durley, of Buttercomb, Yorks, by Elizabeth, dau. Edward Gates. Henry's brother John was a merchant tailor of London.

F. 50^{li}

THEOPHILUS EATON, merchant adventurer. See usual sources.

H. 25^{li}

JOHN ENDECOTT—as yet neither his ancestry nor his profession have been certainly ascertained. See usual sources.

F. 50^{li}

CHARLES FIENNES, son of Thomas, Earl of Lincoln and brother of Theophilus. As he signed the "Humble Request" it is to be presumed that he was an Adventurer. He sailed with Winthrop but returned at once to England.

FRANCIS FLYER, of London, merchant. Son of Matthew Flyer, of London, merchant, by his wife Elizabeth, daughter of John Crouch, of "Cornbury," Herts. Francis Flyer occurs as of Brent Pelham, Herts., and as Francis Flyer, of Roxwell, Essex, he married Martha Boothby, of St. Antholins on 17 April, 1620. His grandfather, Richard Flyer, of Utoxeter, Staffs., married a Cradock of Stafford. He was present 20 October, 1629.

EDWARD FOORD, of London, leather-seller and merchant adventurer of England. He was born at Kynver, Staffs.; the tithes of the school at that place were purchased by the Feoffees for Impropriations. He was

present 15 October, 1629. By his will proved 6 January,
1641 [P. C. C. 2. Cambell (Reg. 45, 161)] he desired
to be buried in the church of Aldermanbury of which
John Stoughton was minister, and he gave "towards the
erecting of a free schoole in New England if anie such
work be done, that the company doeth owe me, which
is in true right fiftie pounds towards that work, which
I value at nothing and yet I am content to give tenn
poundes more towards a free school there to educate
youth, if anie such thing be done." He mentions his
friend Daniel Hodson. [See below.]

F. 50^{li}; FF. 15^{li}; H. 25^{li}

GEORGE FOXCROFT, of London, merchant. Son of Richard
Foxcroft, of Cambridge, by Alice Hodson. In a list
of members of the Fishmongers Company in 1641 he
appears as "merchant of Coleman Street," so he was a
parishioner of John Davenport. He was an Associate
and Assistant in the Charter and one of the gentlemen
in England to whom letters were to be written in 1634.
In 1644 permission was granted to take planks, etc.,
from Foxcroft's estate to pay a debt due by his agent.
[MR. II, 75.]

F. 50^{li}; H. 25^{li}

JOHN GLOVER In Felt's list John Glover occurs and in
    OR   Haven's Joas occurs. Possibly both
JOSSE GLOVER   were subscribers. Josse was the eldest
son of Roger Glover and John, a younger son of the
same, was a "Petter" Barrister of Lincoln's Inn and
married Jane, daughter of Francis Dorrington; there
was also a John Glover, of London, merchant.

For Josse see usual sources.

JOHN: F. 50^{li}; FF. 25^{li}

JOAS: H. 25^{li}

Thomas Goffe, of London, merchant.

Athough appointed Deputy Governor by the Charter there is no evidence that prior to the issue of the Patent he was an Adventurer. He was appointed on a committee 5 March, 1628/9. He was one of the Plymouth Adventurers who sold out to the Planters in 1626. About 1630 he was nearly bankrupt and was pressing for payment of monies due to him. Winthrop instructed his son on 31 August, 1630, not to pay Goffe anything but to require money due; if he refused his bond was to be put in suit. [I, 376.] Humfry laboured to quiet Goffe,—"Though there be a spirit in me that (upon my sufferings from him more than anie) lusts otherwise, yet I dare not give way to it. I have parted with his house . . . much adoo I have to carry myself towards him (being ever vindicating the plantation from his & other mens charges) as to keepe anie faire quarter. I will not trouble you to relate such shrewde collections as hee gathereth from seeing how much adoe your friends & agents here have to supply your present necessities; what (saith he) should I have done or would they (meaning the plantation) if more cattle had come alive, or I had gone on with my Irish voyage; hee saith they seek evasions, not so much because hee hath not performed his part, as because they are not able to make good theirs. Otherwhiles hee will speake and hope all good of and from the plantation; but I wish there may not bee anie occasion given from whence hee or anie may blemish our godly purposes." [*Winthrop Papers*, I, 15.] In 1639 his son Samuel Goffe petitioned the Court for a "competent parcel of ground as well for your petitioners present employment as for his father's benefit." [Lechford, *Note Book*, f. 49.] There is no record that the petition was granted or even received.

MR. 50^{li}

§ JOHN GOODWIN, of East Bergholt, Suffolk, clothier.
By his will, proved 19 June, 1638 [P. C. C. 111, Lee
(Reg. 50, 273)] he left fifty pounds to Matthew Cradock, merchant, of London, to be paid over to the governor of New England to be employed for the benefit
of the Plantation. He mentions John Burges, brother-
in-law of John White, the Rogers family of Dedham and
his kinsmen the Woodgates. [See below.] The sum for
the Plantation is the usual subscription so he may have
been an Adventurer.

ANNE HARVEY.
In 1640 Thomas Browne, of Sudbury, Mass., was
granted 200 acres for Anne Harvey's 25^{li} adventure
[MR. I, 307] and in 1649 William Browne made a claim
on account of 25^{li} put in the joint stock by his aunt,
Mrs. Anne Harvey. [MR. III, 155.]

GEORGE HARWOOD, of London, haberdasher. Son of William
Harwood, of Thurlby, Lancs., by Elizabeth Greenham
and brother of Sir Edward Harwood, Colonel in the Low
Countries, a famous soldier and also a contributor to the
Impropriations Fund. George Harwood was treasurer
of the New England Company and afterwards of the
Massachusetts Bay Company; he was also treasurer of
the "Common Stock," established on the eve of Winthrop's departure, for voluntary contributions, a charitable fund. He was among the gentlemen to be written
to in 1634 and he was asked to render his account in
1638.
E. F. 50^{li}; FF. 50^{li}; MR. 50^{li}

THOMAS HEWSON, of London, merchant.
His name occurs as Huson and Hughesson; the latter
form misled Alexander Young to apply a reference to
Thomas' son to the son of Francis Higginson, who was
only thirteen while John Hughesson had already received

a good education. Huchinson, in his list of the signers of Endecott's instructions, gives him as George in error for Thomas. He supplied 120 flitches of bacon and 120 gallons of sweet oil on 9 March, 1628/9, probably for the ships sailing in April.

> [John Hewson, who supplied shoes and known later as the Cobbler Peer [see Carlyle's *Cromwell*], is supposed to have been his brother.]

Winthrop mentions the arrival of "Mr. Hewson's ship" in a letter of 14 August, 1630; perhaps this was the same shipowner, called Hewes by Hubbard, whose men disputed the possession of Cape Ann with Miles Standish.

E. F. 50^{li}; FF. 15^{li}

FRANCIS HIGGINSON. See usual sources.

JOSEPH HILLS, of Maldon, Essex, woollen-draper.

In a deposition in 1639 he swore that "he came to New England as an undertaker in the ship called the *Susan and Ellen,* of London, in 1635. [Lechford, *Note Book,* f. 91]; undertaker is here used for an Adventurer who emigrated in person. In 1656 he was granted 500 acres "in consideration of an adventure of thirty-three pounds and several services to the country." [MR. IV, 271] (MR. III, 415 gives the sum as 33^{li} 6^s 8^d.) These figures suggest that he had subscribed 100^{li} to the Joint Stock which was drawn down to one-third.

DANIEL HODSON, of London, clothier. Son of William Hodson, of Newcastle, by Emma, daughter of Thomas Kerrey, of Newbury, Berks. [Daniel's brother Thomas was Chancellor of York Cathedral.] Daniel married 1st, Katherine, dau. Edward Saunders, of Bricksworth, Northants., 2nd, Agnes or Anne, dau. Ralph Josselyn, of Roxwell, Essex, widow of Samuel Hutt; at the time of his second marriage he is described as Daniel Hudson,

of Epping, Essex, clothier. She was a cousin of John
Josselyn, who wrote on New England. [Reg. 71, p. 30.]

F. 50^{li}; H. 25^{li}

ATHERTON HOUGH, of Boston, Lincs., gentleman, a parishioner of John Cotton, with whom he emigrated in 1633.
See usual sources. In 1641 he was granted 400 acres
for his 50^{li} adventure.

WILLIAM HUBBARD, father of the historian. See usual
sources.

Hub. 50^{li}

JOHN HUMFRY. See biographical sketch in *Essex Institute
Historical Collections* LXV, 293.

E. F. 50^{li}; H. 25^{li}

THOMAS HUTCHINS.

An Associate and an Assistant in the Charter. He was
present 10 March, 1628/9.

F. 50^{li}; H. 25^{li}; MR. 25^{li}

EDWARD IRONSIDE.

Perhaps he was one of that name who was of Emmanuel
College, Cambridge, incorporated at Oxford 13 July,
1624, and of Lincoln's Inn, 1627. He was licensed by
the Privy Council to travel in 1626. He was present 29
August, 1629.

H. 25^{li}

SIR BRIAN J: ANSON, of London, knt. [? grocer.] Son of
Brian J: Anson by Anne, dau. Robert Lee, of Beacons-
field, Bucks. [The father was 74 in 1633.] He married Mary, dau. Henry Breres, of Lancashire. His
brother John married Thomasine Oldfield, sister of
Joseph Oldfield [see below], and of the other Oldfields
connected with New England. He was appointed an
Assistant in place of Nathaniel Wright at the meeting

at Southampton on 18 March, 1629/30. [MR. 1, 69.] Winthrop writes 22 March, 1629/30: "There is newly come into our company, and sworn an assistant, one Sir Brian Janson, of London, as he hath given 50^{li} to our common stock, and 50^{li} to the joint stock." [*History*, I, p. 367.]

ISAAC JOHNSON.   See usual sources.

An Associate and an Assistant in the Charter.

In 1650, 4200 acres were granted to his executors for his 400^{li} adventure in the Common Stock. [MR. III, 189.] He is said to have adventured 600^{li} [Haven, lxvii] so he may have had 200^{li} in the other stocks. In 1657, 3200 acres were to be laid out for his executors when they had paid 10^{li} due to the country treasurer. [MR. III, 435.]

F. 100^{li}; FF. 25^{li}

ROBERT KEANE, OR KAYNE, merchant tailor. See usual sources as he was famous in "the great sow case."

He was a Plymouth Adventurer who sold out to the Planters. He was one of the gentlemen to be written to in 1634 and he emigrated in 1635. He had 400 acres granted to him in 1639 [MR. I, 262] so had probably adventured 100^{li}.

§ FRANCIS KIRBY.

He is mentioned as a brother of Mr. Downing. He corresponded with John Winthrop, Jr., advising him on the selection of beaver skins and acted as agent, forwarding goods in payment. He was one of the gentlemen to be written to in 1634.

THOMAS LEVERETT, of Boston, Lincs., father of Captain John Leverett; the latter was granted an island off Nahant in 1652, "his father putting in money into the common stock in the beginning of this plantation, for which he never had any consideration." [MR. III, 293.] Thomas

Leverett was associated with Beauchamp in the "Ashley Grant." See Bradford's *Letter Book*, p. 72.

ROGER LUDLOWE.   See usual sources.

There is no record of his subscription; he went out with the Westcountrymen, sailing from Plymouth, and became prominent as an Assistant and Deputy Governor. He was sworn assistant in the room of Samuel Sharpe 10 February, 1629/30.

§ JOHN MALBON, ironworker, "he having skill in iron works and willing to put 25^{li} in stocke, it should be accepted as 50^{li}." [MR. I, 28.] It is not certain that he did subscribe this 25^{li}.

NATHANIEL MANESTY [OR MANESTRY].

There was a John Manesty, goldsmith, of St. Vedasts, Foster Lane, whose will was proved in 1613 [P. C. C. 74 Capell] and who is mentioned in the will of Thomas Palmer [P. C. C. 47 Low], who married Sara, daughter of Vincent Norrington; her sister Anne márried Joshua Winthrop. [Reg. 53, 20.]

Hester Burnell mentions her cousin Lucy, wife of Clement Manistey in her will. [See above.]

There was a Henry Manstie, of Christ Church, London, vintner, will proved 1619 [P. C. C. 115 Dorset], and Elizabeth Mamstey, of St. Botolphs, Bishopsgate, will proved 1625 [P. C. C. 90 Clarke].

ABRAHAM MELLOWS.

Pope, *Pioneers of Massachusetts*, says he invested 50^{li} in the company about 1630. He was granted 200 acres in 1638. [MR. I, 240.]

THOMAS MARSH, of London.

For his adventure of 33^{li} 6^s 8^d he was to have land "according to the proportion agreed on for such adventure," in 1645. One of that name of Allhallows, Lombard Street, citizen and girdler, had his will proved by his son John, 10 December, 1645. [P. C. C. 34 Rivers.] There was a Thomas, son of Robert Marsh, of London, grocer, living in 1634. [*London Visitation.*]

§ PETER MILBURNE, master of the *Arbella*, of St. Dunstans, London. "Mr. Milbourne" took an eighth share in that ship but may not have been an Adventurer, taking it perhaps because he was to be its master.

MATTHIAS NICHOLLS, minister, was in charge of the "Poor's Portion" when John White preached to the Westcountry emigrants at Plymouth in 1630.

In his will, proved 10 October, 1631 [P. C. C. 107 St. John], he writes: "Likewise I give unto the Common Stock for New England, towards the advancement of the plantation, the sum of thirteen pounds." This looks like a subscription of 50^{li} drawn down to one-third. He was a member of the Dorchester Company so was likely to have money in the Joint Stock. For further particulars see "John White."

INCREASE NOWELL.   See usual sources.

He was an Associate and an Assistant in the Patent. He was granted 500 acres in 1638. [MR. I, 262.]

E. F. 50^{li}; FF. 25^{li}; MR. 25^{li}

§ PHILIP NYE, minister, a prominent divine who later became a leading Independent.

He was admitted to the freedom of the Company 25 November, 1628, on his appointment as chaplain but probably never subscribed.

JOSEPH OLDFIELD, son of Roger Oldfield by Thomasine, daughter of John Moore. Of his sisters, Rebecca married John Gearing, one of the Feoffees for Impropriations; Sarah married Josse Glover, see above, and

Thomasine married John J:Anson, see his brother above. Joseph Oldfield subscribed to the Impropriations Fund.

F. 50^{li}; FF. 25^{li}

ABRAHAM PALMER, of London, merchant.

Perhaps related to John Palmer, of London, mercer, who in 1632 left a legacy to the Feoffees for Impropriations. Abraham Palmer emigrated in 1629; he was associated with Elias Stileman as one who was to administer the oath to Endecott. [Haven, Additional Entries.] He was granted 200 acres in 1638. [MR. I, 240.] He went to Barbadoes where he died in 1653.

E. F. 50^{li}; FF. 25^{li}

§ —— PAYNTER.

As "Mr. Paynter" he is mentioned as a benefactor; he may have been related to the Thomas Paynter who was on the first Coroner's Jury in 1630, probably an early settler before Winthrop. [MR. I, 78.] He seems to have been frequently in trouble with the authorities because of his religious views.

HERBERT PELHAM, gentleman. Son of Herbert Pelham, of Compton Valence by Penelope, dau. Thomas, Lord de la Warre, born about 1600. The elder Herbert was half-brother of Elizabeth Pelham, second wife of John Humfry; of Anne, wife of Rev. Edward Clarke, of Fordington, Dorset, and of Thomas Pelham, who married a daughter of Robert Eyre. [For particulars of these relatives and their connexion with the Dorchester Company see "John White."] The younger Herbert married first, in 1626, Jemima, dau. Thomas Waldegrave, of Buers, Suffolk (in the marriage licence he is styled "of Boston, Lincs.") He emigrated to New England where he married Elizabeth, widow of Roger Harlekenden. He returned to England about 1649 and was buried at Buers in 1674. His sister Penelope married Richard Bellingham. (See above.) Four hundred acres were granted to him in 1648 for his 50^{li} adventured in the Common Stock [MR. III, 138] and he took over the interests of his father-in-law, Thomas Waldegrave. He was present 30 April, 1629.

§ —— PEMBERTON. James Pemberton claimed Pemberton's Island and proved in 1652 by the evidence of ancient inhabitants or Planters about the Bay that it had been granted to him above 24 years ago [MR. III, 291]; that is, it was granted in or before 1628 so he came before, or with, Endecott. In a petition of 1640 he states that he had been at Charlestown but had been granted land "on Mystic side." He may have been of the same family as Rev. John Pemberton to whom Lyford wrote of the doings at Plymouth and of Paul Pemberton who left by will in 1625 "my twenty pounds adventured into New England unto the Company [Plymouth Adventurers?] to be employed by them towards the foundation of a church, if ever God give them a settled peace there." [P. C. C. 100 Clarke (Reg. 49, 248.)]

WILLIAM PERKINS, of London, merchant tailor.

His son, Rev. William Perkins, who emigrated in 1631 and settled at Roxbury, was in 1641 granted 400 acres "for his father's 50^{li}." [MR. I, 338.]

RICHARD PERRY, of London, merchant tailor. Son of [Richard] Perry, of St. Petrocks, Exeter. He was an Associate and Assistant in the Charter and frequently attended meetings. He was a prominent Puritan, and a subscriber to the Impropriations Fund. His will was proved 11 January, 1649/50. [P. C. C. 9 Pembroke.] Richard Perry, junior, in 1639 was to be paid 27^{li} long since due, there having been "trouble about it" [MR. I, 270]; perhaps he was the son of the above.

E. F. 50^{li}; FF. 25^{li}; H. 25^{li}; MR. 25^{li}

§ HUGH PETER, minister.   See usual sources.

He was present 11 May, 1629.

E. F. 50^{li}; FF. 25^{li}; H. 25^{li}

§ GEORGE PHILLIPS, minister, of Boxford, Suffolk. See usual
sources. He signed the "Humble Request;" probably
he was employed by the Company and did not subscribe
as an Adventurer.

JOHN POCOCK, of London, woollen-draper. Possibly son of
William Peacock, of London, merchant. He was with
Coulson chosen Assistant *vice* Endecott and Browne, 13
May, 1629. He had been an Adventurer in the Plymouth Plantation and was associated with Shirley in a
claim for goods supplied to the Massachusetts Bay Company; "his fifty pounds" was to be paid to his agent
in corn in 1648. [MR. II, 262.] Lechford mentions
a debt due to him in 1640. He may have been the John
Pococke of Ham Hills, Thatcham, Bucks., whose will
was proved 28 January, 1657/8. [P. C. C. 51 Wootton.]

H. 25^{li}

THOMAS PULISTON, of London, draper. Son of John Puliston,
of Wallington, Flint, by Jane Perry [perhaps sister of
Richard, above]. He married Martha, dau. John
Doughty, of Bristol, alderman. He was present 11
May, 1629.

WILLIAM PYNCHEON.   See usual sources.

He was an Associate and Assistant in the Charter;
present 13 May, 1629. A receipt for his subscription
of 25^{li} is dated 29 August, 1629; possibly it was a second
instalment.

JOHN REVELL, of London, fishmonger.

He was present 28 July, 1629; chosen an Assistant 29
October, 1629, and an Undertaker 10 December, 1629.

He went to New England with Winthrop but returned immediately. He was the only "undertaker" included in the list of gentlemen to be written to in 1634. In a list of members of the Fishmongers Company of 1641 he is said to be resident in St. Nicholas Coleabbey; his membership of that company suggests that he was the "brother-in-law, Mr. John Revell, i.e., half-brother, who is mentioned by Michael Revell, fishmonger of St. Mary Magdalen, Fish Street, in his will proved 8 June, 1659. [P. C. C. 331 Pell.] He was a Plymouth Adventurer.

SIR HENRY ROSEWELL, of Ford Abbey, knt.

He heads the list of Patentees. For an account of him see "John White."

EDWARD ROSSITER, of Combe St. Nicholas, gentleman.

He was chosen an Assistant 20 October, 1629. He was chief of the contingent of Westcountrymen who sailed from Plymouth in 1630. He died 29 November, 1630. For further particulars see "John White."

OWEN ROWE, of London, silk-merchant, or haberdasher, of Allsaints, Honey Lane. He was present 23 March, 1628/. See usual sources.

H. 25^{li}

SIR RICHARD SALTONSTALL, knt. See usual sources.

He was an Associate, Assistant and an Undertaker. He was granted 1000 acres in 1637/8 [MR. I, 222], and many other acres at different dates. 3200 acres were due "for his adventure" in 1645. [MR. II, 132.] He died 7 December, 1672. Haven states that he was the last surviving Patentee.

F. 100^{li}; FF. 25^{li}; MR. 100^{li}

SAMUEL SHARPE, of Trinity Lane, London, merchant.

He acted as agent for Cradock and for the New England

Company. He was appointed a member of Endecott's Council in April, 1630. He was chosen an Assistant 20 October, 1629, but as he was not present to take the oath Roger Ludlowe was appointed in his stead.

Pope, *Pioneers of Massachusetts*, says he sailed with Endecott, but he was obviously in London as late as 10 March, 1628/9 and in October, 1629. [MR. I, 34, 68.]

THOMAS SHARPE, of London, leather-seller; Warden of the Company of Leathersellers in 1641. He was present 3 March, 1628/9 and was chosen Assistant 20 October, 1629. He emigrated with Winthrop but returned, after disasters, in March, 1631. [Dudley's *Letter*.]

§ SAMUEL SKELTON, minister. See usual sources.

He was sent out by the Company and probably never subscribed.

JOHN SMYTH.

Possibly the famous Captain John Smith or he may have been "Mr. Smyth," accountant, who attended a Court on 20 November, 1629.

$$FF. \ 25^{li} + 25^{li}$$

THOMAS SOUTHCOTE, of Mohuns Ottery, Devon, gent.

One of the original Patentees. For particulars see "John White."

JOHN SPENSER, possibly of London. His brother Thomas Spenser of Westminster, in his will dated 22 June, 1648 [P. C. C. Essex 124], refers to his land in New England and bequeathes to his wife and children the wages and liveries due for his "ordinary place of the Guard and Service unto the King's Majesty." [*New England Historical and Genealogical Register*, 44, 390.] See reference to John Spenser, p. 107 above.

WILLIAM SPURSTOWE, of London, mercer. Son of Thomas
Spurstowe, of Shrewsbury, by his wife Katherine. He
married Damaris, dau. Henry Parkhurst, of Guildford,
mercer, by Alice, dau. James Hills, and sister of Sir
Robert Parkhurst; by this marriage he became closely
connected with the Aldersey, Moulson, Coventry, Webb,
Byfield, Cradock and other Puritan and New England
families.

As a member of his congregation he witnessed John
Davenport's signature to the "Articles." By his will,
proved 20 December, 1644 [P. C. C. 26 Twisse (Reg.
52, 158)], he desired to be buried in St. Stephens, Coleman Street, "where I now dwell, by the corpse of my
dear wife," and left legacies to St. Chads, Shrewsbury,
and to poor scholars of Catherine Hall, Cambridge. He
may have been the member for Shrewsbury in the Parliament of 1640. His son, William Spurstowe, was edu-
cated at Emmanuel College, Cambridge, and was a D.D.
from Catherine Hall; he was a member of the Assembly
of Divines and served on the "Committee for Religion"
with Century White. In 1637 he was rector of Great
Hampden, Bucks., and became a chaplain in the Parlia-
mentary Army.

THOMAS STEEVENS, of London, armourer.

Possibly he was related to Thomas Stevens, ironmonger,
who emigrated in 1635.

E. F. 50^{li}; FF. 50^{li}

ELIAS STILEMAN.

He is presumed to have been an Adventurer, as he was
authorized, with Abraham Palmer, to administer the oath
to Endecott. [Haven, Additional Entries, 30b.]

RICHARD TUFFNEALE, of St. Olaves, Southwark, brewer. Son
of Richard Tuffneale. He was a member of Parliament
for Clapham and for Southwark; he married Elizabeth,
dau. and heir of William Humphries, esq., and had a son,

John Tuffneale, of London (knight). Richard's will was proved 1 September, 1640. [P. C. C. 125 Coventry.]

F. 50^{li}; H. 50^{li}

SAMUEL VASSALL, of London, draper. Son of John Vassall, of Ratcliff, of Stepney and of Eastwood, near Roxwell, Essex, by his second wife, born 5 June, 1588. He was an Associate and Assistant in the Charter. See usual sources. He died in 1667.

H. 50^{li}

WILLIAM VASSALL, brother of the above, born 27 August, 1582. He was an Associate and Assistant in the Charter. He emigrated to New England in 1628 but returned in the *Lyon* in 1630. He went again to New England in 1635 and agitated against the autocratic methods of government. He returned to England in 1646 in order to petition Parliament for the liberty of English subjects. About 1650 he removed to Barbadoes where he died in 1655. For the rest see usual sources.

JOHN VENN, of London, merchant tailor. Son of Simon Venn, alias Fen, Lydiard St. Lawrence, Somers., by Maude Lawrence; bapt. 8 April, 1568. He was engaged in the silk and wool trade in the West of England and was Warden of the Merchant Tailors Company in 1641. He was "captain sergeant major" in the Artillery Company and took an active part in the Civil War; he was one of the Regicides and is said to have plundered St. George's Chapel, Windsor, and to have refused to allow a service to be held when Charles I was buried. [See Whichcote below.]

He was an Associate and Assistant in the Charter. In 1644 his son, Thomas Venn, was granted land in regard of his father's money adventured in the Common Stock. [MR. III, 8.]

E. F. 50^{li}; FF. 25^{li}; H. 50^{li}

THOMAS WADE, of Northampton.

His son Jonathan emigrated in 1632 and in 1649 petitioned for land in respect of "60^{li} formerly disbursed by Thomas Wade for his use in the Country Stocke, for the furtherance of this plantation." [MR. III, 154.] This was at first denied but afterwards granted. In 1652 he had 400 acres "with respect to fifty pounds by him formerly disbursed for the use and behoof of the Country," [MR. III, 271], and confirmed because of his "disbursing of 50^{li} for the good of this colony at the first." [MR. IV, 90.]

THOMAS WALDEGRAVE, of Buers, Suffolk. Son of Thomas Waldegrave by his wife Elizabeth, dau. Robert Gurdon, of Assington. He married Margaret, dau. John Holmstead, of Halstead, Essex, and their daughter Jemima married Herbert Pelham [see above], who took over his father-in-law's adventure in the Company and in 1648 received 500 acres for the 50^{li} Waldegrave had adventured. Waldegrave and Pelham were on a committee appointed 30 April, 1629, to frame the oath for Endecott. [MR. I, 39.]

HENRY WALLER, of London.

He was on a Committee 5 March, 1628/9; with one of the Vassalls he objected to having his subscriptions to the Joint Stock drawn down to one-third (see p. 91).

Rev. George Hughes, a noted Puritan divine, then preacher at Allhallows, Bread Street, preached his funeral sermon on 31 October, 1631; this was printed as "The Saints Losse and Lamentation;" in it Waller is described as "the Worshipfull Captaine Henry Waller, the worthy Commander of the Renowned Martial Band of the Honorable City of London, exercising Armes in the Artillery Gardens."

§ NATHANIEL WARD, minister.   See usual sources.

He was employed by the Company so probably did not subscribe.

—— WARREN.

He was present as "Mr. Warren" on 27 April, 1629. There was a Thomas Warren, of London, merchant tailor, son of Edward Warren, of Waterstaff [?], Devon, by Margaret, dau. Ambrose Searle, of Godford, Awliscombe, of which latter place John Maverick was vicar, and there was a Thomas Warren whose daughter Mary married John Younge, probably of St. Margarets, Southwold, Suffolk, minister, who emigrated to New England, and there was a Richard Warren, of Fordington, Dorset, whose daughter Joan married Ralph Sprague and with him emigrated in 1628.   [See "John White."]

GEORGE WAY, of Dorchester, Dorset, glover.

He was a member of the Dorchester Company; for full particulars see "John White."

F. 50^{li}

FRANCIS WEBBE.

He was present 2 April, 1629, and was interested in establishing a mill near Salem; John White recommended this task to the Company. He married a sister of Samuel Aldersey. He is mentioned in the will of Margaret Hill, of Banbury, Oxon., in 1656, in which place John White's sister Elizabeth Allen also resided.

Pope, *Pioneers of Massachusetts*, says he was granted 200 acres on 28 September, 1640.

[Hutchinson says *Thomas* Webbe signed Endecott's *Instructions* but this is doubtless a slip for Francis.]

E. F. 50^{li}

NICHOLAS WEST.

He signed the Cambridge Agreement but there is no evidence that he emigrated as agreed.

SIMON WHETCOMBE, of London and Sherborne, woollen merchant. He was probably a member of the Dorchester Company in place of his brother Robert. He was one of the original Patentees. For particulars see "John White."

F. 50^{li}; FF. 25^{li}; H. 85^{li}; MR. 25^{li}

CHARLES WHICHCOTE, of London. Son of Christopher Whichcote, Esq., by Elizabeth, dau. Edward Fox. His sister Elizabeth married George Foxcroft [see above] and his brother Richard married Judith, sister of George Foxcroft. His brother Benjamin married Rebecca, widow of Matthew Cradock and of Richard Glover.

It is said that Colonel Charles Whichcote as Governor of Windsor Castle, refused to allow the Prayer Book to be used at the burial of Charles I—"the Common Prayer Book was put down and he would not suffer it to be used where he commanded." [See above John Venn.]

F. 50^{li}; H. 50^{li}

EDMUND WHITE, of St. Lawrence Jewry, Esq. [? haberdasher.] He was a member of the Haberdashers Company, had a brother John, of Patrickborne, knt., and held property in Powick, Worcs. His will was proved 19 February, 1632/3. [P. C. C. 14 Russell (Reg. 48, 135.)] Possibly he was the father of James White, a wealthy merchant of Boston, Mass.

JOHN WHITE, Utter Barrister, of Lincolns Inn.

He was present 19 October, 1629. For particulars see "John White," where the reasons for distinguishing him from his name-sake are given.

JOHN WHITE, minister, of Dorchester, Dorset. For full particulars see "John White."

E. 50^{li}

RICHARD WHITE.

Possibly Richard White, master of the *Peter of Way-mouth*.

MR. 25^{li}

DANIEL WINCH.

Probably son of Daniel Winch, of St. Mildreds Poultry, grocer, who was buried in that church 19 March, 1624/5 [his will P. C. C. St. Cleere], and of Sibill Winch who contributed to the Impropriations Fund in 1631. She was buried in St. Mildreds 2 November, 1631. Her son Robert Winch proved her will. [P. C. C. 117 St. John.] This Robert married a granddaughter of Roger Oldfield; Thomasine (Oldfield) J: Anson mentions him in her will as the husband of her niece and leaves legacies to their children Daniel and Rebecca. This marriage connected the Winches with the Glovers, Winthrops and others (See above.) Robert was a silkman of Cheapside and is mentioned with Vassall as a member of the Drapers Company in the will of Samuel Penoyer in 1652. [Reg. 45, 157.] He was most probably brother of Daniel the Adventurer.

H. 25^{li}

JOHN WINTHROP.   See usual sources.

Mentioned as on a Committee 19 September, 1629. His 200^{li} in Joint Stock had not been fully paid up on 5 April, 1630. [*History,* I, p. 371.]

—— WOODGATE.

"Mr. Woodgate" was present 28 July, 1629. John Goodwin (see above) married Elizabeth Woodgates, of East Bergholt, who had brothers Thomas and John living in 1625.

NATHANIEL WRIGHT, of London, merchant. Perhaps son of
John Wright, of Romford, Essex.

He was an Associate and Assistant in the Charter;
was present 2 March, 1628/9. Haven points out that he
is not to be confused with Dr. Nathaniel Wright, physician to Oliver Cromwell, who also prescribed for his
friend John Winthrop and was a friend of Israel Stoughton. [See above, p. 125.] These two Nathaniels were
probably related.

H. 25^{li}

SIR JOHN YONGE, of Colyton, knt.

An original Patentee. For particulars see "John
White."

JAMES YOUNG, of London, merchant. Perhaps son of James
Young, of Bristol, merchant; both were living in 1633.

He was an Undertaker, appointed 10 December, 1629.

RICHARD YOUNG, of London, haberdasher. Probably son of
Henry Young, of Poulton-cum-Seacombe, Cheshire, by
Margery, dau. Robert Gill. He was present 6 April,
1629. He contributed to the Impropriations Fund in
1625. John Tod on 10 May, 1648, was granted 100 acres
in consideration of the adventure of Mr. Richard Young
[MR. II, 246.]

Attention is called to the close family connexion between many of the Adventurers and the common interest
they possessed; five inter-related groups can be formed,
the same name occurring in more than one, and as in
many cases they prove to have been acquainted before
the Company was established, it may well be considered
a "close corporation" of relatives and friends.

The titles adopted below are somewhat arbitrarily
chosen but they will serve.

THE FAMILIES GROUP. By marriage were related: Aldersey, Thomas Andrewes, Burnell, Crane, Crowther, Flyer, Foxcroft, Glover, J: Anson, Manisty, Oldfield, Spurstowe, Webbe, Winch, Whichcote, James Young. To these may be added others who were either emigrants or closely associated with the Company: Byfield, the Lord Keeper Coventry, Eyre, Hubbard, Moulson, Offspring, Parkhurst, Ratcliffe, Rogers, Wyn. Perhaps there was a cousinship between Harwood, son of Elizabeth Greenham and Cradock, son of Dorothy Greenham

THE ROXWELL GROUP: The three Brownes, Flyer, Hodson, Pelham, Pyncheon, Vassalls, Waldegrave—to these may be added Eliot, Josselyn and Josias, brother of John White.

THE IMPROPRIATIONS GROUP: ? Aubrey, Aldersey, Eyre, Richard Andrewes, Davenport, Davis, Foord, Harwood, Oldfield, Perry, Richard Younge, with Bridges, Gearing and Offspring.

THE DORCHESTER GROUP: Bushrod, Darbie, Humfry, Nichols, Pelham, Southcote, Way, Whetcombe, White, Sir John Yonge.

THE EASTERN COUNTIES GROUP: Bellingham, Coddington, Downing, Dudley, Fiennes, Hough, Hubbard, Humfry, Johnson, Kirby, Nowell, Pelham, Winthrop and all the Earl of Lincoln connexion.

Other groups may be formed by the reader himself— such as the Merchant Group, and the rest.

BIBLIOGRAPHY

Adams, C. F. *Three Episodes of Massachusetts History.*
      1896.
——, J. T. *The Founding of New England.* 1921.
Bradford, William. *History of Plymouth Plantation,* ed. Ford.
      1912.
—— *Letter Book,* Massachusetts Historical Society Collec-
      tions. 1st Series, III.
—— *Letter of 8 September, 1623;* see American Historical
      Review, VIII.
Browne, Alexander. *The Genesis of the United States.* 1890.
Cromwell, Letters and Speeches of, ed. Carlyle. 1845.
Dudley, Thomas. *Letter to the Countess of Lincoln.* Force
      Reprint.
Essex Institute Historical Collections. Vol. LXV.
Felt, Joseph. *Annals of Salem.*
Goodwin, J. A. *The Pilgrim Republic.* 1888.
Gorges, Sir Ferdinando. *Brief Narration.* Maine Historical
      Society, Vol. II.
Haven, S. F. *American Antiquarian Society Transactions,*
      III.
— *Early History of Massachusetts* (Lowell Lectures).
Higginson, Francis. *A True Relation.*
Historical MSS. Commission, XII. App. II.
Hubbard, William. *History of New England.*
Hutchinson, Thomas. *History of Massachusetts.* 1795.
Lechford, Thomas. *Note Book.* 1885.
Massachusetts Historical Society Collections, 2nd Series, IV.
                                        5th Series, I.
Massachusetts Historical Society Proceedings, 1869/70.

New England Historical and Genealogical Register.
Newton, A. P. *Puritan Colonization.*
Osgood, H. L. *The American Colonies in the 17th Century.*
    1904.
Pope, Charles H. *The Pioneers of Massachusetts.* 1900.
Prince. *Chronology of New England.* 1736.
Records of the Council for New England. Ed. Deane.
    American Antiquarian Society Proceedings. 1867.
Records of the Governor and Company of Massachusetts. Ed.
    Shurtleff.
Scott, W. R. *Joint Stock Companies.*
Smith, Captain John. *Generall Historie of Virginia.* 1623.
State Papers Colonial, Calendar of. Vols. V, VIII.
Thornton, J. Wingate. *The Landing at Cape Anne.* 1854.
White, John. *The Planters Plea.* Force Reprint.
Winsor, Justin. *Narrative and Critical History of America.*
Winthrop, John. *History of New England.* Ed. Savage.
    1853.
——, R. C. *Life and Letters of John Winthrop.* 1864.
Winthrop Papers. Massachusetts Historical Society Collec-
    tions. Series 5, Vol. VIII.
Wood, Anthony à. *Athenæ Oxoniensis.*

INDICES

INDEX OF NAMES

167

INDEX OF PLACES

INDEX OF SUBJECTS

175

Lightning Source UK Ltd.
Milton Keynes UK
UKOW040020290512

193490UK00012B/62/P